The Essence of
TAO

The Essence of
TAO
PAMELA BALL

EAGLE EDITIONS

Published by Eagle Editions Limited
11 Heathfield
Royston
Hertfordshire SG8 5BW

This edition published 2004

Copyright ©2004, Arcturus Publishing Limited
Unit 26/27 Bickels Yard
151-153 Bermondsey Street
London SE1 3HA

ISBN 1-84193-189-6

Printed in India

Contents

Contents

Preface

When I first began to study the *Tao Te Ching* some thirty years ago, I was a young housewife looking for a system of belief that fitted in with some of my own radical ideas. In the intervening years many people have given their own rendering of the original texts. It is to these people that I must express my gratitude, because they have enabled me to write this book and reveal the beauty of a text that is still my constant companion. The students and disciples of Tao have left a legacy of belief and practice for which we are all the richer.

I would like to draw your attention to two aspects of this book before you begin. Firstly, something needs to be said about spellings. Chinese scholars differ tremendously in the spelling of important names and words and it is difficult for the lay person to decide which is the more accurate. Throughout this book I have chosen those spellings that fit in with the limited understanding that I possessed when I first studied Tao. I have attempted to be consistent throughout, but that does not mean – in the true spirit of Tao – that any one is more right or wrong than the other. My spelling of key words is given below and, to help you in your research, some alternative spellings are shown in brackets. For the sake of simplicity, I have also italicized all foreign words and book titles.

Chuang Tse (alternatives Chuang Tze, Chuang Tzu, Zuang Zi)
Chi (alternatives *Chi, ch'i*)

Chi Gung (alternatives *Chi Kung, Qi Gong, Qi Jong*)
Ching (alternatives *Ch'ing, ching, Jing*)
Lao Tse (alternatives Lao Tze, Lao Tzu)
Tai Chi (alternatives *T'ai Ch'i, tai chi*)
tan tien (alternative *dantien*)
Tao (alternative Dao)
Tao Te Ching (*Dao de Jing, Dao De Jing, Dao de Zing, Tao te Ching*)

Secondly, pertinent quotations have been chosen and placed at the end of each chapter for the reader's consideration. The selections are purely arbitrary and – in the spirit of Tao – are not meant to prove any particular point. They might, however, be used in one of several ways: as food for thought; as a focus for meditation; or as the basis for a daily prayer. Because the Tao is so adaptable you will find that you are able to use the quotations in whichever way works best for you.

Introduction

Though words or names are not required
to live one's life this way,
to describe it, words and names are used,
that we might better clarify
the way of which we speak,
without confusing it with other ways
in which an individual might choose to live.

Before we even begin to think about understanding the concept of Tao we have to appreciate that it was in existence long before anyone tried to explain or describe it.

In all the translations of, and the writings about, the Tao (when spoken, 'Dao') there is an insistence that words and names are superfluous, that the Tao – while apparently having no objective reality of its own – can only be experienced subjectively. It is a philosophy, a pursuit of wisdom and a study of natural realities. Tao is *not* a religion: that is Taoism. We must, however, use words to explain how Tao came to be written down, what part it played in history and what its relevance is in the modern world.

Tao is such a universal principle, a way of living, that we are wiser to understand it than learn it. The ideas that Tao conveys, which have given rise to some of the most effective poetry in the world, are more important than the words or characters used. The Chinese written language uses forms that describe ideas and Jung interprets the Chinese character for Tao thus:

> a track which, though fixed itself, leads from a beginning directly to the goal.

Tao itself is most often translated as 'the Way', and often we find our own Tao when we least expect it. This is because this principle of life – this flow of cause and effect – has been around us the whole time without our noticing it. Only when our attention is drawn to it do we realise that it is an integral part of our lives and that we can do nothing else but walk 'the path of life' in front of us.

Just as we think we have begun to understand a part of that path, the flow of information shifts like water (another meaning of 'Tao') and we are presented with a new puzzle, a different conundrum for consideration. In the present-day Chinese language, the character for Tao has as many as thirteen meanings. Some of these meanings were not in use when the *Tao Te Ching* (also known as *Dao De Jing*) – the first scripture and the definitive essence of Tao – was transcribed in the sixth century BC. We shall explore the legend of its writing later.

Tao is a principle which, when we learn to follow and to feel it, gives us the opportunity to be in harmony with the world in which we live and with Nature. The more we are in harmony, the easier it is to prolong or preserve life. Because Tao is paradoxically both the ultimate source of all things and also its many manifestations, as we become more aware so we become conscious of the duality of everything.

Its essential nature is such that we are continually being presented with paradoxes: if it is the void (no-place) it is also the energy within that void; if it is pure energy then no-thing can contain it. For us to comprehend the process of creation we must understand that, simply, Tao exists and yet also gives rise to everything created. In this there is an awesome sense of the miraculous and a strong sense of beauty. To be able to access fully the beauty of Tao, we need to understand the meanings behind the title of the *Tao Te Ching* and some of the words used.

Te is most easily translated as 'Virtue' or 'Power'. A Taoist meaning for *Te* is 'Tao within'. It is virtue in the sense of the attributes needed in order to experience Tao – those which are inevitably brought to the fore and enhanced in any attempt to work with Tao. This process of development gives the individual power over his own shortcomings and therefore creates in him the power of control over the world in which he lives. This concept is demonstrated by a fairly recent translation in a verse of the *Tao Te Ching*:

> The Master doesn't try to be powerful;
> thus he is truly powerful.
> The ordinary man keeps reaching for power;
> thus he never has enough.

In many ways *Te* is simply that which we require in order to live our lives within the Tao; as such, *Te* suggests correct performance as we tread the path of life. We have to develop the integrity to adhere as closely as we can to the tenets of Tao if we are to maximize our own potential, yet each individual can only act in accordance with their understanding of what Tao represents. It is our relationship with Tao that decides our actions.

The prime requirements for following Tao are a life of simplicity, communion with nature, denial of selfishness and a mystical union with the Ultimate. These lead to the establishment of three qualities – compassion, reserve or frugality and humility – which, in the *Tao Te Ching*, are called 'treasures'. These treasures help us to understand others, accept what we cannot change and maintain our equilibrium no matter what transpires. The following translation expresses the idea in this way:

> He who knows other men is discerning; he who knows himself is
> intelligent.

He who overcomes others is strong; he who overcomes himself is mighty.

He who is satisfied with his lot is rich; he who goes on acting with energy has a (firm) will.

He who does not fail in the requirements of his position, continues long; he who dies and yet does not perish, has longevity.

The Three Treasures are really all that are needed to follow the Tao and yet they are very difficult to put into practice. Which of them we find most difficult will depend on our innate personalities. The answer to this difficulty is to adopt the idea that striving is unnecessary and that non-action is the right response, particularly insofar as our worst attribute is concerned. The Chinese word for this is 'wu wei'. In this context wu wei does not mean inaction (doing nothing), but rather a chosen course of deliberately not doing anything – allowing the matter to unfold.

The best example of this is seen in what today has been called 'peak experience'. Let us suppose that you are trying to make a tennis ball land on a chosen spot. The more you try to do this the less possible it seems. If you relax and do not consciously try you will find that you then begin to succeed at your chosen task. Although you are doing something (hitting the tennis ball) you are also carrying out non-action – sometimes known as not-action – in that if you hit the spot that is fine and if not it doesn't matter. When you consistently hit the target you are in line with Tao, and your universe is co-operating with you.

The external world is fragile,
and he who meddles with its natural way,
risks causing damage to himself.
He who tries to grasp it,
thereby loses it.

Introduction

The recommendation to 'Do nothing, and do everything' is based on the strong belief, held by those who study the Tao, that Man interferes with the entirely natural course of events. Most of the ills of society have been the result of the deliberate waywardness of Man, who has frustrated the cosmic order of things. The solution to this problem is not to attempt to control events but to resign one's will to the Tao and so become an instrument of its eternal way. By this method one returns to the *Te* (virtue) of the Way.

The word '*Ching*' has the general meaning of 'Classic' when translated from Chinese into English. The ching is authoritative, comes from the sages and cannot be contradicted, only commented upon. It echoes the basic meaning of Tao in that it is unwavering, unchanging and eternal. A further meaning of *ching* is 'essence', so *Tao Te Ching* might be translated as 'The Classic Way of Virtue', 'The Virtues of the Way of the Sages' or even the 'Essence (basics) of the Right Way'.

Complicating matters even further, in order to understand even more fully the complexity behind Chinese thinking, we also need to comprehend the core belief that *Ching* may be translated as semen, spermatozoa and one of three essential life forces. The other two forces are the breath, or vital energy (*chi*), and the mind or consciousness (*shen*). These three forces or energies must intermingle to a greater or lesser degree in order to achieve the preservation of life. In his *Pao-p'u-tzu*, the Taoist alchemist Ko Hung says:

> Man is in *ch'i* and *ch'i* is within each human being. Heaven and Earth and the ten thousand things all require *ch'i* to stay alive. A person that knows how to allow his *ch'i* to circulate (*h'sing-ch'i*) will preserve himself and banish illnesses that might cause him harm.

Because Tao is such a complete way of life it has attracted many adherents throughout its history and there are many schools of thought associated with it. The idea of physical immortality, for instance, goes back to the very beginning of Taoism and its attainment is the aim of most schools of religious Taoism (*tao-chiao*). Some of these schools are the alchemical School of the

Outer Elixir (*wai-tan*), Way of Right Unity (*Cheng-i tao*) and the Five Pecks of Rice Taoism (*wu-tou-mi tao*).

As soon as various sets of beliefs become associated with philosophical thought, that thought inevitably loses some of its purity; and when rituals and practices are introduced in order to achieve the desired goals, that philosophy becomes a religion – often with an attendant hierarchical structure. This is largely what happened to followers of the Tao, as we shall see in Chapter 5.

We do need to keep reminding ourselves that Tao is both a universal principle and an individual way of being and the original scriptures help us to do this admirably. While the definitive scripture is undoubtedly the *Tao Te Ching* there are others which are equally important. The chronological order of the initial scriptures is:

> *The Tao Te Ching:* Written by Lao Tse, there are eighty-one chapters which are often divided into two parts – the Book of Tao (Chapters 1–37) and the Book of Te (Chapters 38–81).

This is the definitive exposition of Tao and is probably the one on which all others are based, since the others are separated from this by some 200 years.

> *Chuang Tse* (or *Zuang Zi*): Written supposedly by Chuang Tse and others, there are seven inner and twenty-six miscellaneous and outer chapters.

This is the second most important Taoist scripture written initially by Master Chuang (Zuang) in a more humorous vein than the *Tao Te Ching*. It contains many anecdotes that illustrate points made by the authors.

> *Lieh Zi:* Attributed to Lieh Zi it contains 111 chapters.

This emphasizes the certainty of our annihilation, resigning oneself to fate and avoiding too much effort in life.

Introduction

Hua Hu Jing: by an unknown author, it is claimed that this scripture is a collection of eighty-one chapters of the 'lost' writings of Lao Tse. Thought to have been banned for many years, there is some controversy over its authenticity.

Chinese scholars would add many more writings that are probably beyond the scope of an introductory book such as this, though it is important to appreciate how the *Tao Tsang*, or Taoist canon, came into existence. Through these scriptures, it is possible to appreciate how other religions, particularly Buddhism and Confucianism, developed along with Taoism in China.

Chinese philosophy in Taoism is mystical and intuitional, somewhat similar to Western Mystical religions, whereas Confucianism has been said to be a hundred times more rationalistic than Western philosophy: Confucian ethics are certainly clear and uncompromising. Buddhism with its Four Noble Truths – all to do with the handling of Suffering – and its strong connections with magic and folklore satisfied many who were neither mystical nor of a rational turn of mind. Later Taoism owed much to the blending of Buddhist thought and ceremony.

Present-day philosophers are fortunate to have at their disposal the thoughts and writings of their predecessors of all persuasions and it is refreshing to discover that the tenets and ideas of Tao have given inspiration to many deep thinkers. It is somehow comforting to know that the unchanging force which was perceived so clearly over two thousand years ago still makes itself felt to those who wish to experience it.

Nowadays, the Tao still requires as pure a vessel as possible for its energies to function properly. If we use the analogy of a boat we can see that both inwardly and outwardly we can be buffeted by all sorts of difficulties in life. In making ourselves responsible for our own progress it behoves us to aim for the best physical and mental state that we are capable of, with the ultimate aim of a kind of spiritual discipline. *Chi Gung, Tai Chi* and other forms of exercise all are designed to achieve correct movement and flow, initially within the physical realms but later within the spiritual.

Introduction

Healing and alchemy, within the framework of the Tao, have their place in attaining the correct balance in life and achieving a stable yet dynamic force or power within. This is represented by the principle of Yin/Yang (positive/negative). The ancient systems of divination such as the *I Ching* (Book of Changes) – which actually predates the written *Tao Te Ching* – are more properly manuals of correct action and ways of bringing about a balanced viewpoint. They therefore form part of the knowledge of the Tao.

Continuing with the analogy of a boat, to understand Tao we must consider the principle of Emptiness. Earlier we spoke of *wu wei*, which is doing no-thing. Emptiness means doing nothing except leaving space – leaving room for the flow of energy simply to happen. If we do not stand in our own light or in that of others, that vessel which is our physical being can travel without difficulty through the vicissitudes of life. Equally, if we can allow space within ourselves, we have room for new energy and new power which moves us in the right direction.

We can achieve that emptiness or space through the use of meditation and visualization. The primary hallmark of Taoist meditation is the generation, transformation and circulation of internal energy and this requires some considerable practice. The two primary guidelines in Taoist meditation are *jing* (stillness and calmness) and *ding* (concentration and focus). Within that focused stillness, both mental and physical, we can reach a totally undisturbed and transformative state of mind, which permits intuitive insights to arise of their own accord, by concentrating the mind and directing our awareness.

You will be given the opportunity to experience some Taoist meditations and techniques later. When you have achieved this particular state of being you will have found and experienced your own Tao and will, it is to be hoped, no longer use or need words to describe it. You will have travelled a full circle.

Chapter One:

What is Tao?

*I do not know
its name.
If I must assign a word to it
I call it Tao.*

The Tao can be explained as 'the reason or cause of everything that followed on from it'. This sentiment is reiterated many times within the myriad of extant translations of the original explanation of the Tao. Tao, as the source of everything, undoubtedly existed before the philosopher Lao Tse — whose birth is traditionally assigned to the year 604 BC – came to write down his understanding of it. Indeed many of the physical disciplines and ideas were in existence in China before they were brought under the umbrella of Taoist belief. Lao Tse's scriptures allowed others to grasp the principle, and thus today many regard Lao Tse as an interpreter, rather than the instigator, of the system of belief.

As a philosopher, Lao Tse was also an observer both of human beings and the natural phenomena around him. He concluded that behind all these manifold workings of Nature there exists an Ultimate Reality which in its essence is unfathomable and unknowable and yet manifests itself in recurring laws of abiding regularity; for example, the sun rises and sets, plants grow and are harvested, man lives and dies.

This Essential Principle had no name, so he tentatively called it Tao, although he realized that naming it was not only inadequate but certain restrictions were also immediately introduced. Here he came up against a difficulty experienced by other people who have tried to describe this Essential Principle (there are those within the Jewish religion who will not speak the name of God for this reason). In the Muslim religion God is given 99 names. There are of course more than 99 names for God, but 99 in Arabic carries the inherent idea of 'many'; as does the term 'Ten Thousand' when used to describe the Tao.

The modern word that best illustrates this difficulty is perhaps 'Godhead', a term used to describe a motivating and ordering principle within the universe. This idea moves the average Westerner away from the concept of a personal god into a much more numinous and all-pervading principle which Lao Tse called Nature.

What is Tao?

It is said that Lao Tse became disenchanted with the work that he was doing as archivist in the Chouh Imperial Court and determined to journey to the West in order to follow his own Way. Asked by the border guard to write down his understanding of Tao so that others could follow his teachings, he inscribed some 5,000 characters divided into eighty-one chapters. The characters are open to interpretation according to the individual level of understanding that has been reached by the reader, but taken together they represent basic tenets which enable a person to live fully within the framework of the natural forces around him.

In his book, *The Secret of the Golden Flower*, Carl Jung describes the Chinese character for Tao as follows:

> The character of tao in its original form consists of a head, which probably must be interpreted as *beginning*, and then the character for *going* in its dual form in which it also means *track*, and underneath, the character for *standing still*, which is omitted in the later way of writing.

This description gives us, in a slightly more flowing form, the idea of starting out on a track which involves standing still. As a philosophical argument this is beautiful, since one must decide whether the track or the individual stands still! A modern day image might be that of a travelator at an airport. We are able to stand still and yet at the same time be carried to our destination. If we choose we can walk along it but must then take care to accommodate ourselves to the movement under our feet.

So it is with Tao. Once we choose to begin our journey then it is up to us to act appropriately at all times in order to make the best use of the power available to us. Looking at this slightly more esoterically, we have a path which has been there from the beginning of time and requires only our will to travel in that way. The chapters of the *Tao Te Ching* (the Book of Tao), particularly the first thirty-seven, give information on what is required for us to travel most efficiently and effectively.

Chapter One

Translations and Interpretations

From the turn of the 20th century onwards, when the original texts become more available to the West, the Book of Tao has lent itself to translation and interpretation. One recent example, rendered by Peter Merel in a rather poetic fashion is:

> Embracing the Way, you become embraced;
> Breathing gently, you become newborn;
> Clearing your mind, you become clear;
> Nurturing your children, you become impartial;
> Opening your heart, you become accepted;
> Accepting the world, you embrace the Way.
>
> Bearing and nurturing,
> Creating but not owning,
> Giving without demanding,
> This is harmony.

Below is a much more literal translation by James Legge written in 1891. He was the renowned translator and transmitter of the Chinese Classics to the Western world. It is he who entered the words in brackets to clarify the meaning:

1. When the intelligent and animal souls are held together in one embrace, they can be kept from separating. When one gives undivided attention to the (vital) breath, and brings it to the utmost degree of pliancy, he can become as a (tender) babe. When he has cleansed away the most mysterious sights (of his imagination), he can become without a flaw.

2. In loving the people and ruling the state, cannot he proceed without any (purpose of) action? In the opening and shutting of his

gates of heaven, cannot he do so as a female bird? While his intelligence reaches in every direction, cannot he (appear to) be without knowledge?

3. (The Tao) produces (all things) and nourishes them; it produces them and does not claim them as its own; it does all, and yet does not boast of it; it presides over all, and yet does not control them. This is what is called 'The mysterious Quality' (of the Tao).

Finally, for comparison, we give a translation from Peter Muller:

Pacifying the agitated material soul and holding to oneness:

Are you able to avoid separation?
Focusing your energy on the release of tension:
Can you be like an infant?
In purifying your insight:
Can you un-obstruct it?
Loving the people and ruling the state:
Can you avoid over-manipulation?
In opening and closing the gate of Heaven:
Can you be the female?
In illuminating the whole universe:
Can you be free of rationality?

Give birth to it and nourish it.
Produce it but don't possess it.
Act without expectation.
Excel, but don't take charge.

This is called Mysterious Virtue.

We can see that the principle on which all these translations are based is simple enough – that of complete 'transparency' in all things – but the application of the principle in everyday life is surrounded by difficulties, not least the understanding brought by the translators themselves. The images of simplicity, such as the infant, echo the Christian precept of becoming 'as little children' in understanding and the idea of 'cleansing the sight' suggests the development of inner vision seen in the practice of yoga. Such ideas are pointers for those who are capable of comprehending them.

We have to 'get hold of Tao' – understand – for ourselves. This means putting aside any preconceived ideas that we might have and listening to the simple truth behind the scriptures. We also have to be able to feel that truth. In the examples quoted above, each of the translators gives Lao Tse's instructions quite clearly. The 'mysterious quality' of the Tao (harmony) is manifested in the individual who understands the principle of accepting that you can allow things to happen naturally without interference.

Old Master Lao Tse speaks such universal truths in his scriptures that while it would be difficult to suggest that this great system of philosophy belongs only to him – that he is its 'father' – we can at least give him credit for recording his thoughts and musings in ways that free the mind from its self-imposed limitations, even in today's busy world.

Lao Tse was not content to be purely and simply a philosopher. He was aware that man could model himself on Tao – that he was a reflection of the greater whole. In this way, possibly without intending to do so, Lao Tse put himself in the position of becoming a social reformer: his influence was not only felt in his own culture but in those that came afterwards.

In the second part of his scriptures Lao Tse expounds the virtues or 'Three Treasures' that are necessary in order to be able to follow Tao. We shall consider these shortly, but first, in order to show how Lao Tse's writings were interpreted by his followers, we should consider the writings of Chuang Tse. He lived some 200 years after Lao Tse and therefore had the writings of Confucius available to him as well.

All profound thinkers attract the notice of a particularly able follower who sets out to interpret the thoughts and writings of their master, therefore imposing their own style and thoughts on the basic teaching. This is not peculiar to followers of the Tao – which actually encourages free interpretation – but is seen in many other schools of thought. Jesus was followed by the more restrictive St Paul, Socrates by Plato and Confucius by Mencius. The original master writes little or nothing while the disciple often writes long and profound treatises.

This was so in the case of Chuang Tse. He uses many more apocryphal stories and examples than Lao Tse and introduces an element of wry and contemplative humour which was perhaps lacking in Lao Tse's writings. We give an example of one such story below.

> Hui Tse said to Chuang Tse, 'I have a big tree named ailanthus. Its trunk is too gnarled and bumpy to apply a measuring line to, its branches too bent and twisty to match up to a compass or square. You could stand it by the road and no carpenter would look at it twice. Your words, too, are big and useless, and so everyone alike spurns them!'

> Chuang Tse said, 'Maybe you've never seen a wildcat or a weasel. It crouches down and hides, watching for something to come along. It leaps and races east and west, not hesitating to go high or low – until it falls into the trap and dies in the net. Then again there's the yak, big as a cloud covering the sky. It certainly knows how to be big, though it doesn't know how to catch rats. Now you have this big tree and you're distressed because it's useless. Why don't you plant it in Not-Even-Anything Village, or the field of Broad-and-Boundless, relax and do nothing by its side, or lie down for a free and easy sleep under it? Axes will never shorten its life, nothing can ever harm it. If there's no use for it, how can it come to grief or pain?'

Chuang Tse asks continually that we perceive the ordinary and mundane in a different way. He makes no mention of Divine Principle, of the purpose of being, or personal immortality, simply that we return to the flow. This is such a basic principle in belief in the Tao that it leaves room for a sense of the ridiculous. The only philosophical tool he uses is logic, therefore he can make fun of anything which strikes him as 'ridiculous' in that particular moment. This ability ultimately enables the individual to consider his immortality.

Chuang Tse believed that life is transitory but also dynamic and constantly changing, a viewpoint which led him to the belief that self-transformation is central to the practice of Tao. He had no interest in those people who sought wealth and personal aggrandizement; he preferred to observe and understand the world and always to consider the paradoxes which life presented. In his writings he asks:

> Do the heavens revolve? Does the earth stand still? Do the sun and
> the moon contend for their positions? Who has the time to keep
> them all moving? Is there some mechanical device that keeps them
> going automatically? Or do they merely continue to revolve,
> inevitably, of their own inertia?

Seeing Nature at work and the way in which anomalies arose had him musing on causal factors and he came close to the idea of a being with responsibilities:

> Do the clouds make rain? Or is it the rain that makes the clouds?
> What makes it descend so copiously? Who is it that has the leisure
> to devote himself, with such abandoned glee, to making these
> things happen?

In the Tao, where all dualities are eventually resolved into unity, it is up to the 'wise man' to recognize what part he plays in the order (and ordering) of things in the universe.

Perhaps one of the best-known conundrums presented to us by Chuang

Tse is the butterfly dream. Here he deals with the issue of the interchangeability of appearance and reality and with duality. Perhaps also he deals with altered states of consciousness. He says:

> Once I, Chuang Tse, dreamed I was a butterfly and was happy as a butterfly. Suddenly I awoke, and there was I, visibly Tse. I do not know whether it was Tse dreaming that he was a butterfly or the butterfly dreaming that he was Tse.

The butterfly is today a symbol of the soul, so Chuang Tse was aware that even in our dreams we may become capable of interpreting different levels of our own reality. It depends on the point of perception (where we are coming from) which viewpoint we accept. He recognizes how the man of knowledge must act and says:

> The sage has the sun and the moon by his side. He grasps the universe under his arm. He blends everything into a harmonious whole, casts aside whatever is confused or obscured, and regards the humble as honourable.

Like Lao Tse he makes no judgement about people, but differentiates between the return to the source of all things as an action and the flow to source as an inaction. Wu wei as the principle of Emptiness, of non-doing, is central to the Taoist belief system.

As a philosopher Chuang Tse subscribes to no particular school of thought apart from perhaps that of Chaos. He says:

> I am energy
> I am Tao
> I am
>
> I

THOUGHTS AND IDEAS

As an author, words obviously are important to me.
However, it is only when we realise that each word whether spoken or
written creates a particular vibration that they have even more meaning.
Some of the following quotations are chosen because they express that
sentiment, others because inherent in them is the sense of economy of
movement and power important to those who study the Tao.

When I use a word, Humpty Dumpty said, in a scornful tone,
it means just what I choose it to mean – neither more nor less.
The question is, said Alice, whether you can make words mean so
many different things.
The question is, said Humpty Dumpty,
which is to be master – that's all.
Alice was too much puzzled to say anything.
Lewis Carroll
Alice Through the Looking Glass

So here I am, ... having had twenty years –
Twenty years largely wasted..
Trying to use words, and every attempt
Is a wholly new start, and a different kind of failure....
...And so each venture
Is a new beginning, a raid on the inarticulate
With shabby equipment always deteriorating
TS Eliot
Four Quartets
(East Coker Quartet, Lines 172-180).

Acceptance
Harmony is only in following the Way.

The Way is without form or quality,
But expresses all forms and qualities;
The Way is hidden and implicate,
But expresses all of nature;
The Way is unchanging,
But expresses all motion.

Beneath sensation and memory
The Way is the source of all the world.
How can I understand the source of the world?
By accepting.
Peter Merel's interpolation

It is said "Someone caused it" or "No one did it", but we are thus debating about things and the end is that we shall find we are in error. We may speak and we may think about it, but the more we speak, the wider we shall be off the mark. When you look for their origin it goes back to infinity, when I look for their end, it proceeds without termination. The name Tao is a metaphor, used for the purpose of description. Neither speech nor silence is sufficient to convey the notion of it.
Alan Watts

High Virtue is non-virtuous;
Therefore it has Virtue.
Low Virtue never frees itself from virtuousness;
Therefore it has no Virtue.
High Virtue makes no fuss and has no private ends to serve:
Low Virtue not only fusses but has private ends to serve
John C H Wu

That which is called the Tao is not the Tao

The flow of energy.....
Here.......
It.......
Is.......

Nameless......

Timeless......
Speed of light......

Float......beyond fear.....
Float......beyond desire

Into...this Mystery of Mysteries
Timothy Leary
Psychedelic Prayers

Chuang Tse

'Consciousness wandered North to the land of the Dark Waters and climbed the Unnoticeable Slope, where he met Speechless Non-Doer. " I have three questions for you," consciousness said. "First, what thought and efforts will lead us to understanding the Tao? Second, where must we go and what must we do to find peace in the tao? Third, from what point must we start and which road must we follow in order to reach the Tao?"

Speechless Non-Doer gave him no answer.

Consciousness travelled South to the land of the Bright Ocean and climbed the Mountain of Certainty, where he saw Impulsive Speech-Maker. He asked him the same questions. "Here are the answers," Impulsive Speech-Maker replied. But as soon as he started to speak, he became confused and forgot what he was talking about.

Consciousness returned to the palace and asked the Yellow Emperor, who told him, "To have no thought and put forth no effort is the first step towards understanding the Tao. To go nowhere and do nothing is the first step towards finding peace in the Tao. To start from no point and follow no road is the first step towards reaching the Tao.

Chapter One

Complete Spirit

Chi Hsing Tzu was training a fighting cock for the King.
After ten days he was asked if the bird was ready, and he said, 'Not
yet. He's still vain and quarrelsome, and relies on his own spirit.'
After another ten days, he said, 'He isn't ready yet. He's still alarmed
by the appearance of another bird.'
After ten days more, he replied, 'No, Not yet. He still looks fiercely,
and is full of spirit.'
When the fortieth day had passed, he replied to the question,
'Nearly ready. Though another cock crows, he doesn't react in the
slightest. To look at him, you would say he was a cock made of
wood. His inner quality is now complete. He has no need to fight,
because no other cock will dare to confront him.'

Yao wanted to cede the empire to Hsü Yu. 'When the sun and
moon have already come out,' he said, 'it's a waste of light to go on
burning the torches, isn't it? When the seasonal rains are falling, it's a
waste of water to go on irrigating the fields. If you took the throne,
the world would be well ordered. I go on occupying it, but all I can
see are my failings.
I beg to turn over the world to you."
Hsü Yu said, 'You govern the world and the world is already well
governed. Now if I take your place, will I be doing it for a name? But
name is only the guest of reality - will I be doing it so I can play the
part of a guest? When the tailor-bird builds her nest in the deep
wood, she uses no more than one branch. When the mole drinks at
the river, he takes no more than a bellyful. Go home and forget the
matter, my lord. I have no use for the rulership of the world! Though
the cook may not run his kitchen properly, the priest and the
impersonator of the dead at the sacrifice do not leap over the wine
casks and sacrificial stands and go take his place."

Chuang Tse in *Spiritual Teachings of the Tao* by Mark Forstater

Words that are simple but profound in meaning are good words.
Principles that are condensed but comprehensive in application
are good principles.

Not to speak with a man who can be spoken with is to lose a
man. To speak to a man who cannot be spoken with is to waste
words. He who is truly wise never loses a man, he too, never
wastes his words.

Chapter Two:

Tao and Nature

Man places himself in harmony with his body
His body tunes itself to the slow unfolding of life
Life flows in harmony with the Tao.

The principle of Energy is very simple. It is a dynamic interchange between two polarities which creates power – today recognized as a simple electrical principle. The Chinese discovered, without giving it a name, that this simple principle seemed to act within the universe and resulted in the creation of all things. They understood that Nature required a balance between two polarities in order to exist. This they called the Yin/Yang Principle, or *Tai Chi*. This 'reason or cause of everything', the principle of Energy, they named Tao.

If Tao is Energy, Taoism might be defined as a set of beliefs which enables us to live successfully within that Energy; indeed, ultimately to recognize that we can become that Energy. As a consequence, Tao becomes a way of living in accordance with natural laws, living as Nature intended. In today's world this can be particularly difficult when we are beset by modern technology and all the desires, illusions and possessions that it generates. The first requirement of Tao then is living as simple a life as possible and for that we have to go back to basics, to the beginning.

Starting from the philosophical viewpoint that Tao is the beginning, the point of origin common to everything, there equally have to be universal processes for manifestation and realisation. Arising from that common beginning are a myriad of expressions, each one being unique. Having said that, there do seem to be certain laws which are applicable to all those expressions and to the interrelationships between them.

The Taoist will do his best to discover and understand those laws, conform to them as much as possible and find the best 'fit' for himself within the scheme of things. Ideally, he has no need to interfere in that scheme. If he does deem it necessary to do so, he will do as little as possible to disturb the status quo. When he trusts the processes of the universe he is able to accept that he is part of those processes and will co-operate with them rather than trying to control them.

Thus when a Taoist, or rather one who follows Tao, finds himself in a particular situation or context, he is able to take an overview, for he knows he does not exist in isolation. He is able at one and the same time to see why the situation has arisen, what needs to be done and what will be the consequences of any action that is taken.

The *Tao Te Ching* expresses this concept thus:

> Empty yourself of everything.
> Maintain a steady serenity.
> All things take shape and become active,
> but I see them return to their source,
> like vegetation that grows and flourishes,
> but returns to the root from which it springs.
>
> Returning to the source is serenity;
> it is to realize one's destiny.
> To realize one's destiny is to know the eternal.
> To know the eternal is to be enlightened.

Not to know the eternal
is to act blindly and court disaster.

More prosaically there is a nursery rhyme which expresses this concept in a
somewhat humorous manner:

Big fleas have little fleas upon their backs to bite 'em.
Little fleas have littler fleas
And so on ad infinitum.

Exploration and experimentation leads the Taoist to conclude first of all that
everything in Nature is inter-related. From that comes the knowledge, through
observation of those interrelationships, that all phenomena have a time and
place to occur, interact and evolve. Life is cyclical in Nature; there is growth
and decay which in turn is followed by growth. The law of the Tao, reflecting
natural order, states that everything returns to its starting point. Anything that
develops to its extreme will invariably revert to the opposite qualities. The *Tao
Te Ching* states:

Reversion is the movement of the Tao.

Taoism carefully observes then calculates these natural laws, experiments with
the findings in order to prove the hypotheses by further observation and
finally confirms those natural laws and all the implications. It therefore might
be called a qualitative science.

Traditional Chinese science has, in many ways, been more successful than
its Western counterpart in bringing light to bear on the workings of Nature,
perceiving the latter purely and simply as a unified energetic force. This is why
in the most modern physics of the universe, quantum field theory, the
universe itself can be described through analogy as a still and transparent
ocean of energy with all existing manifestations being waves within it.

How we experience that ocean of energy will depend upon our

perspective. From the ocean's perspective it contains everything. From the perspective of the waves – if we were the waves – we would experience our individuality as a movement. Were we to experience ourselves as the water of the ocean we would be conscious of the fact that we permeated both the waves and the ocean, that we were the essence of them both. It would be difficult however to experience ourselves as all three at once.

Although we call them physics and biology, the same laws of Nature and the different perspectives that we deal with today were observed by the scientists and practitioners of the Han period in China (second century BC), when Taoism was first being written down. They set up their various systems of correct *feng shui* (environmental management), exercises such as *Tai Chi* and *Chi Gung* (designed to strengthen their links with their internal energy) and meditation and inner 'alchemy' (to enhance their relationship with natural forces) in such a way that their own essence or chi was given the maximum opportunity to express itself as fully and perfectly as possible.

The Taoists, in accordance with given knowledge, found it easy to categorize phenomena around them in terms of the Five Elements – Water, Fire, Wood, Metal and Earth – and particularly in terms of *yang/yin* (positive and negative). (We shall study this categorization more fully later in the book since it is such an integral part of living within the Tao.) The expressing of chi became somewhat subverted into the pursuit of longevity in the later 'Fire' traditions which are more active, whereas the 'Water' traditions – as laid down by Lao Tse – remained more able to allow things to happen at their own speed. It is this difference in the use of energy that marks the essential division between Philosophical Taoism and Religious Taoism, and between dynamic stillness and the martial arts.

The Taoist Water tradition – based on carrying out every preparation possible so that one is open to all that goes on – had been in existence for over a thousand years before Lao Tse wrote down, almost as a code of conduct, the *Tao Te Ching*. It is a classically practical way of allowing the mind and body to release or dissolve its blocked energy and allow the essential energy (*chi*) to flow and be itself for as long as possible. As we shall see later, this follows the course of natural laws in its cyclical nature; daily, within the seasons and within the management of the physical body.

In the Water tradition in which the energy flows – literally like water – whatever we do must feel comfortable, but without strain. Using all our effort, not using force and harming neither body, mind or spirit requires perhaps even more self-discipline than any martial art. At the same time it is a very gentle method which allows individuals to find their own essential being, their light – that part which never changes – and allows them to be confident and grounded within the world in which they exist. Their light is a 'cool' one however and their mysticism is concerned with the nature of human beings and how they relate to the universe. For the Taoists who practise the Water tradition everything is transient: it comes and it goes. They have a mind of their own and at least some degree of control over their own destiny. Ultimately, their goal is internal alchemy, a natural change within themselves. The Fire tradition is somewhat different, in that it is far more active and the use of force is an integral part of its teaching. It is possible to push the mind and body to its limits, for the end justifies the means. The Fire methods can be quite cathartic, for the power generated will quite literally 'blast through' any blocked energy. This can be seen in many of the martial arts practices where the energy is used more externally and somewhat explosively.

Visualization is often used as a very effective tool, and magical practices or *chi chi guai guai* ('when strange things happen') become a potent part of the practitioner's armoury. The power that he thus discovers is a hot energy or light and his mysticism is more about how he relates to his universe. He is capable of manipulating energy and matter, though this can be quite hard on the nervous system. Just as fire purifies metal, so the idiosyncrasies of the ego are burnt away and both inner and outer transformation takes place.

Many Taoists nowadays practise a blend of Water and Fire methods which is entirely appropriate in today's frenetic world. Sometimes it is right to allow problems to dissolve and there is no need to take action – one keeps one's own counsel and waits. At other times action may be required, when one acts quickly and then withdraws again into obscurity. No one method is more right than another but the practitioner must know and understand himself very well in order to use both methods. Many Taoists are accustomed to developing their own practice in the light of that understanding and tend not to have very much to do with other organized religious bodies.

However, there is a basic core to all Taoist practice, expressed in Chinese as *Ching Chi Shen Wu Tao*, part of which we have already explored. *Ching* is the life-force which gives rise to *Chi*; *Chi* is vital energy which gives access to *Shen*; *Shen* is Spirit which achieves *Wu*; *Wu* is Emptiness which leads to *Tao* – the root of all things. This progression, however, is not linear, but is cyclical and it is this that allows us to understand the workings of Nature.

Working on this premise, the basic life-force becomes *Chi*, a manifestation of energy. This energy permeates everything and is the aspect of life that is worked with most by the Taoist. When *Chi* becomes stable and is no longer chaotic it begins to become more refined and ultimately gives access to *Shen*, or Spirit. When the Taoist practitioner achieves this state of awareness, there is a sense of connectedness with the natural world and a depth of perception which means becoming conscious of the natural flow of life. There is a feeling of belonging and a profound sense of reality. The practitioner has little sense of time or space; one of the apparently more negative aspects is that nothing matters any more.

In reality, we move through this feeling until it becomes a sense that nothing consists of matter, that everything is illusion and that there is no substance to anything. This is the basic life-force putting itself in touch with Emptiness. The paradox is that as everything is nothing, so it is also everything. In other words, there is actually no difference between being no-thing and being every-thing.

Normal everyday life has a way of interfering with this perception and it becomes quite difficult to hold on to the concept. It is this concept of *Wu* (Emptiness) that is so central to Taoism. The aspect of *wu-wei* (doing nothing) is thus not so much taking no action, but understanding Emptiness. There are truly no words to describe this, which in turn brings us back to Lao Tse's words:

> If I must assign a word to it
> I call it Tao.

The interesting thing is that as you experience Emptiness and allow your energy to move through to experiencing the Tao, there is a duality present. There is the individual that is having the experience and the Tao that is external to the individual. This perception introduces the idea that you are 'this' and Tao is 'that'.

Immediately we say Tao is 'that' but not 'this' we have moved away from being able to make a proper definition or achieve a proper understanding. As soon as we recognize that Tao is ineffable (beyond description) – that it just 'is' – we can allow it to 'be' and can concentrate on its multiple manifestations, including ourselves.

Nature is also a manifestation of the elusive Tao. Tao is both everywhere and nowhere and we can learn to live in harmony with Nature in all its forms. Looked at in a purely rational manner this is impossible, so we have to suspend disbelief and try to achieve Emptiness, simply allowing Energy the freedom to flow through us.

> The Way takes no action,
> but leaves nothing undone.
> When you accept this,
> The world will flourish
> In harmony with nature.

> Nature does not possess desire.
> Without desire, the heart becomes quiet;
> In this manner the whole world is made tranquil.

In some senses pure Energy is chaotic and yet beneath that chaos is a feeling of order, an order that can become apparent given the right opportunity. No Western word precisely describes the concept of Tao which is why, when

Western philosophers try to explain it, some of the explanations can be extremely idiosyncratic. Tao in its purest form is potential. It does not do anything or actively produce something, it simply 'is'. It is without form and without shape, but at any given moment it is flowing and changing. As it begins to give itself form, it again becomes the seed of life (*ching*).

For the people of Ancient China who lived almost exclusively off the land, the idea of nurturing the seed of life in all its forms was obviously very important. Most families were extremely self-sufficient, so the family structure was important: each member had a fairly proscribed set of tasks and duties which helped the families to remain independent.

The people referred to their homes as '*tien, yuan, lu mo*' which meant 'fields, gardens, houses and graves'. All of these contained the seed of life and therefore, by extension, also contained spirit or spirits. Disturbing these spirits could have a very harmful effect on the health and safety of the family, therefore the families took tremendous pains to remain in harmony with these spirits and used amulets, spells, prayers and incantations in order to placate them. Because of this, the home was not just limited to the current living members but also included the wisdom of the ancestors and the potential of the future. Lengthy travel was generally avoided so that the tranquillity of the individual and his environment was not disturbed more than was absolutely necessary.

The rigid hierarchical structure within the family later expanded into the government of the country with very strong precepts about authority and respect. In a patriarchal society there was a great danger of corruption and Lao Tse's wise words about the sage's (wise man's) conduct gave voice to ideas of the government of the people.

> Throw away holiness and wisdom,
> and people will be a hundred times happier.
> Throw away morality and justice,
> and people will do the right thing.

Throw away industry and profit,
and there won't be any thieves.

If these three aren't enough,
just stay at the centre of the circle
and let all things take their course.

As traditional family values were modified to create a reduced dependence on the immediate home and family, Taoism provided a direction and a way of conducting oneself so that happiness could be achieved. This meant that one could remain neutral and did not have to take sides in any conflict or argument. It would be possible to adopt the Middle Way.

The Middle Way indicates achieving a balance between positive and negative – *yang/yin*, a natural law. So we return again to a very simple principle of action when action is necessary, and non-action when appropriate. In a simple society, this way of being is very natural; for example one rises with the sun and sleeps when it is dark. While the *Tao Te Ching* advocates an ideal way of being, in modern times this is somewhat more difficult to achieve: in many ways the external natural laws are more difficult to follow. We cannot all gain a living from the land, nor can we necessarily stay within the close environs of our immediate surroundings. We must all interact with other people in different ways.

E-mails and other modern forms of communication would have seemed miraculous to the ancient Chinese, who would perhaps have suspected evil spirits. Today, the way of internal alchemy, that of bringing about changes in our consciousness in accordance with the old laws, gives us mastery over the 'evil spirits' of electromagnetic energy, chemicals, pesticides and other modern discoveries.

The idea of living simply and according to Nature means different things to different people. We all have the freedom to live according to the tenets of the Tao in whatsoever way we deem suitable. The basic disciplines remain the same, whenever and however they are applied.

The rise in the quest for (and consumption of) organic produce within season; the search for spiritual knowledge; the awareness of Man's responsibility towards all other forms of life on the planet; and the development of a sustainable future for mankind are all aspects, whether we realize it or not, of living within the Tao. It is but a short step to recognize that allowing ourselves to do so without hidden agendas, or a desire for any particular outcome – to be empty – is truly living within the Tao.

When we are prepared to recognize that to be 'immortal' is to allow our energy to flow and be part of the greater whole, we have achieved the potential to be 'beings of light'. To be within the Tao, on a practical level, means that we need to clarify the various levels of our existence and work with them both individually and jointly in the most effective way possible. This truly becomes a way, or philosophy, of life.

THOUGHTS AND IDEAS

The quotations that follow speak of those things that are natural or within the flow of Nature. I have chosen them because they seem to me to epitomise the power of the natural that we are all searching for within our lives. The picture of two old men having the time to stand and argue over what a fish feels is to my mind particularly appealing.

As we begin to live our lives within the flow of Nature we have more time to consider the philosophical questions of life.

Swimming Free

Chuang Tse and Hui Tse were walking on the bridge over the River Hao, when Chuang Tse said "Look how the fish come to the surface and swim around so freely –
that's what they really enjoy!"
Hui Tse said "You're not a fish. How do you know what makes a fish happy?" Chuang Tse responded "You're not me. So how do you that I don't know what fish enjoy?"
Hui Tse said "I'm certainly not you, and so I don't know what you know, but your are definitely not a fish, and that proves that you don't know what makes fish happy."
Chuang Tse replied "Let's return to your original question. You said to me 'How do you know what makes a fish happy?' You already knew that I knew it, when you put the question to me. And I know it because of how you and I enjoy ourselves strolling freely together on this bridge."

Chuang Tse in '*Spiritual Teachings of the Tao*' by Mark Forstater

Support

In mythical times all things were whole:

All the sky was clear,

All the earth was stable,

All the mountains were firm,

All the riverbeds were full,

All of nature was fertile,

And all the rulers were supported.

But, losing clarity, the sky tore;

Losing stability, the earth split;

Losing strength, the mountains sank;

Losing water, the riverbeds cracked;

Losing fertility, nature disappeared;

And losing support, the rulers fell.

Rulers depend upon their subjects,

The noble depend upon the humble;

So rulers call themselves orphaned, hungry and alone,

To win the people's support.

The best of man is like water,

Which benefits all things, and does not contend with them,

Which flows in places that others disdain,

Where it is in harmony with the Way.

So the sage:

Lives within nature,

Thinks within the deep,

Gives within impartiality,

Speaks within trust,

Governs within order,

Crafts within ability,

Acts within opportunity.

He does not contend, and none contend against him.

Form is a revelation of essence.
As the drop becomes the ocean, so the soul is deified, losing her
name and work, but not her essence.
You must break the outside to let out the inside: to get at the
kernel means breaking the shell. Even so to find nature herself all
her likenesses have to be shattered.

If trees are felled day after day on a hillside it becomes denuded.
So it is with the human heart. Given a chance, it regenerates.

A tree as big around as you can reach starts with a small seed; a
thousand mile journey starts with one step.' Wisdom, Happiness
and Courage are not waiting somewhere out beyond sight at the
end of a straight line; they're part of a continuous
cycle that begins here. They're not only the ending,
but the beginning as well.

Who accepts nature's flow becomes all-cherishing;
Being all-cherishing he becomes impartial;
Being impartial he becomes magnanimous;
Being magnanimous he becomes natural;
Being natural he becomes one with the Way;
Being one with the Way he becomes immortal:
Though his body will decay, the Way will not.

The Way is limitless,
So nature is limitless,
So the world is limitless,
And so I am limitless.

Nature says only a few words:
High wind does not last long,
Nor does heavy rain.
If nature's words do not last
Why should those of man?

Who accepts harmony, becomes harmonious.
Who accepts loss, becomes lost.
For who accepts harmony, the Way harmonizes with him,
And who accepts loss, the Way cannot find.

The Kui envies the millepede, the millepede envies the snake the
snake envies the wind, the wind envies the eye,
and the eye envies the mind.
The Kui said to the millepede, "I have this one leg that I hop along
on, though I make little progress. Now how in the world do you
manage to work all those ten thousand legs of yours?"
The millepede said, "You don't understand. Haven't you ever
watched a man spit? He just gives a hawk and out it comes, some
drops as big as pearls, some as fine as mist, raining down in a
jumble of countless particles. Now all I do is put in motion the
heavenly mechanism in me –
I'm not aware of how the thing works."
The millepede said to the snake, "I have all these legs that I move
along on, but I can't seem to keep up with you who have no legs.
How is that?"
The snake said, "It's just the heavenly mechanism moving me
along – how can I change the way I am?
What would I do with legs if I had them?"
The snake said to the wind, "I move my backbone and ribs and
manage to get along, though I still have some kind of body.

But now you come whirling up from the North Sea and go whirling off to the South Sea, and you don't seem to have any body.

How is that?"

The wind said, "It's true that I whirl up from the North Sea and whirl off to the South Sea. But if you hold up a finger against me you've defeated me, and if you trample on me you've likewise defeated me. on the other hand, I can break down trees and blow over great houses – this is a talent that I alone have. So I take all the mass of little defeats and make them a Great Victory. To make a Great Victory – only the sage is capable of that!"

Chapter Three:

Tao and Taoism

But knowing harmony creates abstraction,
and following abstraction creates ritual.
Exceeding nature creates calamity,
and controlling nature creates violence.

As time goes on, the philosophy of Taoism is becoming increasingly popular, particularly as other religions experience difficulties in attracting followers. It is still resistant to any sort of classification, however, purely and simply because it has a history of adaptation and change in line with its origins as philosophical thought. These thoughts, which give a blueprint for living life successfully, are seen as being as relevant today as they were when Taoism was first organized as a religion in the first century AD.

From that time onwards, the religious practices of Taoists were very much geared to attaining wisdom and longevity in the here and now, not at some moment in the future which would give them a life in the hereafter. It was recognized, however, that the requirements of those who did attain such heights were different to their fellow men, and that they needed the rarified atmosphere of sacred spaces. The later alchemical practices suggested that the true follower of the Tao was capable of creating that sacred space within himself. This of course fits in very well with the Western concept of New Age living, giving a fertile ground for the further study of Tao.

Chapter Three

A *History of Taoism*

The history of Taoism can be divided into four separate periods:

1. Philosophical or Proto-Taoism
2. Classical Taoism
3. Modern Taoism
4. Contemporary Taoism

It is important not to allow any one of these periods to take precedence over another nor, as is sometimes done, to try to see any of the periods as a kind of progression from the last. That would be against the very nature of Tao, which responds to the needs of the times and grows of itself generically. It is true to its basic tenet of continuous change.

The first period, Philosophical or Proto-Taoism, is so called simply because there is no evidence of any formal Taoist religious organizations at this time – from antiquity up to the second century. The classic works of philosophy that were written during this time, the *Tao Te Ching* and the *Chuang Tse* in particular, while extremely influential in the formation and growth of the later classical Taoist tradition, were in fact texts of their time, when people were looking for explanations. In the first case, explanations were required for some very difficult concepts which had been around for some time in the *I Ching* or Book of Changes. In the second, explanations were required of the explanations and this was done through allegory and humour. There was no 'ism' as such, just followers of the Tao.

The second period, that of Classical Taoist religion, starts in AD 142 when the first successful organized Taoist religious system was instigated by Chang Taoling, who later, as a deity, was given the title *Tien Shih*. This system was intended to refocus the misguided religious practices of the majority of the people, and reinstate original ideas. Because the original Taoist scriptures were much more philosophical in nature, some way was needed of marrying the simpler beliefs of the people with the loftier ideals expressed. Chang Taoling was said to have received his knowledge from the by now immortal Lao Tse and the system was known as the 'Way of the Celestial Masters'. It addressed the spiritual needs of the community, including seasonal ceremonies.

This school was skilled in the use of talismans, amulets and magical practices. Taoist priests today still claim to be ordained in a lineage that stretches back to this original founder (he is also claimed as one of their founders by the Five Pecks of Rice sect – so named from the 'fee' paid for healing or prayers).

Two other important movements developed later from this early organization: the Way of Highest Clarity (*Shangqing* – also Shang Ch'ing –Taoism) and the Way of Numinous Treasure (*Lingpo* or *Lingpao* Taoism). At the end of the Northern Sung (AD 960–1126) dynasty the Celestial Masters school was strengthened by the then Celestial Master, Chang Chi-hsien – as a result of his work the movement came to be known as the Way of Orthodox Unity (*Cheng-i Tao*). Chang himself became known as Chang the Immortal.

At around the same period as the original Celestial Masters, the Taoist 'religion' developed in another area of the Chinese empire, yet despite their similarities the two strands appear to have had no direct connection with each other. Chang Chueh, who died in AD 184, founded the Taoist school of *T'ai-ping Tao* (Way of the Supreme Peace). His teachings are based on the doctrines of the *T'ai-p'ing ching* and stem from the *Huang-Lao Tao* (Way of Huang-ti and Lao Tse). These teachings were designed to create supreme peace, with everyone having the right to a peaceful existence through the establishment of equality for all, including the healing of sickness.

At a time when the land was torn by famine and there was considerable oppression from those in authority, this ideal brought him a great deal of acclaim. Chang Cheuh's healing rituals in pure chambers (*Chih shih*) amassed him a following of several hundred thousand followers. Between AD 165 and AD 184 eight provinces had accepted his teachings. He organized his followers into a hierarchical structure along military lines, with himself at their head as celestial duke-general. In AD 184 he led the rebellion of the Yellow Turbans against the Han dynasty – which was ruthlessly put down – during which he and his brothers, Chang Pao and Chang Liang, were killed. Thus the Way of Supreme Peace was ultimately caught up in a good deal of violence.

The period between the second and the seventh centuries marks an era during which many Taoist practices, texts and rituals took shape. During that time, Buddhism was brought to China by missionaries from India and Tibet, and although there were periods of intense rivalry between Taoists and Buddhists, many of the latter's ideas and practices were absorbed into Taoism.

The *Ch'ing-tan* Neo-Taoist school of the time also shows some Buddhist influence. This school practised a refined form of conversation on the philosophical teachings of the Tao and also reinterpreted the Confucian classics, holding that Confucius was a greater Taoist than either Lao Tse or Chuang Tse because he actually achieved a state of non-being.

The *Lingpo* tradition in particular was strongly influenced by Mahayana Buddhism. The most important elements that were brought to bear on Taoist doctrine were the Buddhist emphasis on personal transgression or sin, based on a highly structured cosmology with nine layers of hell, and the Buddhist dogma of the kalpa (cyclical period) of the decline of the universe. The Shangqing tradition on the other hand was much more strongly influenced by shamanic practices that involved adept journeying to the stars to encounter various deities. This was highly intriguing to a people already versed in an understanding of the cycles of nature.

It was during the Tang dynasty (AD 618–906), which – from the perspective of the development of art and culture – is one of the most important times in Chinese civilization that Taoism became fully integrated with the Imperial Court system. The term '*Shangqing*' itself refers to the Heaven of Highest Clarity inhabited by celestial immortals of the supreme rank. It therefore suited the hierarchical structure of the court. There are four important themes evident in their scriptures:

1. the knowledge of the deities belonging to the Big Dipper constellation who are the closest to the 'Supreme Ridgepole' (*Tai chi*) around which the heavens revolve.

2. the governance of *Fengdu* (the underworld) by a central administration that decides the fate or destiny (*ming*) of human lives.

3. absorbing the spiritual essence (Light) of the sun and the moon refines the physical body until it is capable of becoming a 'being of light'.

4. the gods each have their own realm within the human body and can be visualized there.

Thus Taoism exerted, at this point, complete supremacy over Buddhism particularly under the reign of the Xuanzong Emperor (AD 713–756).

The period known as Modern Taoism begins with the Song Dynasty (AD 960–1279). When considering this period, it is extremely difficult to separate out Taoism as a religious category because the boundaries between the various religions and cults become somewhat blurred over time. That is not to say that Taoism disappeared altogether, for this era saw the development of sects named 'Supreme Unity' (*Taiyi*), 'Perfect and Great Tao' (*Zhenda Tao*), and 'Complete Perfection' (*Quanzhen*). Indeed, many contemporary and modern accounts actually portray the twelfth century as a particularly innovative period for Taoists.

The Way of Complete Perfection is the major monastic form of Taoism that, even today, exists alongside the more practical priesthood of the Celestial Masters. The Way of Complete Perfection details the perfection of the practice of internal alchemy. Here, the energies of the body are finely tuned and developed through breathing techniques and other forms of meditation. These energies are then in turn transmuted into more and more subtle forms, thus giving the potential for longevity and even, it is hoped, the ability to transcend death itself.

The Way of Complete Perfection became highly influential under the Mongol Yuan dynasty after the founder's disciple Qiu Changchun (AD 1148–1227) undertook a three-year journey to the court of the warlord Genghis Khan. While the aim throughout this time appeared to be the coordination of the teachings of Confucianism, Taoism and Buddhism there were many discordant arguments with Buddhists. When the Taoists lost a series of these arguments many Taoist texts were destroyed or burned. Taoism on the whole continued to flourish during the subsequent Ming dynasty (AD 1368–1644) and by AD 1445 the compilation of the Taoist Canon (*Tao Tsang*), a compendium of some 1,500 Taoist texts, took place under the patronage of the Yongle Emperor.

Later still, during the Qing dynasty (AD 1644–1911), Taoist ideas and practices became more obviously ingrained in popular religious culture. From that time on, Taoist practices and arts such as *Tai Chi Chuan, Chi Gung* and *Feng Shui* became increasingly widespread.

	Traditional Religious Taoism	Contemporary Taoist thought in the West
Deity	Those who have achieved immortality, depending on historical period, including the Three Pure Ones and the Eight Immortals	Tao students and practitioners have a more spiritual focus, the Tao being impersonal, and not in the image of god or man
Creation	The Universe began when *chi* ('breath') separated into Yin and Yang. Taohua is used to mean 'Creation without a Creator'	Recognise that the creation process was regulated by Tao, as one became two became three then many, but the process itself is unknown and unknowable
Communion with the Divine	Divination, magic, external alchemy, shamanic mediation, rituals and rites, adherence to the *Tao Tsang*	An inner alchemy through introspection, meditative practices, personal transformation according to Taoist concepts of peace, harmony and emptiness
Morality	Dictated by the body of work known as the *Tao Tsang* and received knowledge	Dictated generally by the *Tao Te Ching*, and revealed personally from within, through meditation
Afterlife?	No, although the sage could become physically immortal by practicing special meditations and eating certain foods	Not specifically, except by transcending and acceptance of death through knowledge of and being in Tao
Texts/Scriptures	*Tao Tsang (Taoist Canon), The Three Caves* and *Four Supplements*, and sometimes the *I Ching*	*Tao Te Ching*

The fourth period in China, that of Contemporary Taoism has, particularly since 1949, been a difficult time for Taoism as a religion. During the period of the Great Proletarian Cultural Revolution (1966–1976) many Taoist temples were destroyed and the religion to all intents and purposes ceased to exist in mainland China, except as a somewhat archaic curiosity. However, in line with most sets of beliefs which have been heavily persecuted, it has not been possible to destroy it completely, and since 1980 Taoism has begun to be practised openly once more in China. To those who choose to follow the Way there is little or no difference between the sacred and the secular and a new generation of Taoists are labouring to rebuild their places of worship and to resurrect their traditions.

At the same time, as people in the West continue to search for meaning in their lives and to look for valid alternatives to conventional religious systems, Taoist temples, enclaves and study groups have been more widely established in Europe, the Americas and elsewhere. The fascination with all things Oriental, because of the emigration of many Chinese people across the world, has resulted in an upsurge of Taoist-based practices such as *Chi Gung* and *Tai Chi Chuan* (also known as *Tai Chi*). The need to understand the philosophical thought and belief behind these practices has therefore taken root in the West. So we have a return to the original philosophical concepts as laid down in the *Tao Te Ching* and the writings of Chuang Tse as separate from the religiosity of the Immortals and Taoist deities. The study and practise of Tao and its associated beliefs is beginning to thrive once again in China and throughout the world.

The term 'Philosophical Taoism' has come to mean something slightly different to the original concept in the present day. The original writers of the scriptures were thinkers and philosophers who practised a particular way of life that was right for their time. Research, the finding or revealing of lost texts and a deeper understanding of the moral makeup and mysticism of the Chinese people has led to a comprehension of the impulses behind the writings which may be successfully applied to the present day. The Philosophical Taoism of Lao Tse and Chuang Tse strives for spiritual immortality; that is, enlightenment and the attainment of oneness with the highest principle (Tao).

It does need to be said, however, that what was written probably meant one thing to the writers, was understood in a different way by each reader, was translated again differently for the Western mind and interpreted in a fourth way by the modern mind. As with anything which arises from a creative impulse, the scriptures speak to those who need them: for those to whom they do speak they are a source of inspiration and meaning.

The same might also be said of the religion of Taoism, although for different reasons. The system of belief in the immortals and deities which bring comfort to the Chinese mind will not necessarily have the same effect for the Western personality, so in the pursuit of knowledge one must be discriminatory.

Unless one has an appreciation of magical practice, for instance, one can have no concept of the *ch'eng-huang* – the protective deity of a city. These deities ward off disasters and protect the inhabitants of their cities. The tradition dates back to ancient times and was adapted by Taoism, which admitted these city protectors to the ranks of its most important deities. Their feast day was an important festival and was celebrated with parades at which a statue of the *ch'eng-huang* was carried through the streets. The ch'eng-huang also act as guides to the souls of the departed. A Taoist priest who undertakes to help the soul (*hun po*) of a dead person out of Hell must inform the protective deity of the city by submitting a document seeking permission.

This is only one example of a Taoist belief. Individual faith must inevitably be formed as much by relevant ritual and practice as by scripture. So, for those who follow the Tao today there is much to be learned – not just from the ancient Canons but also from modern day writers and philosophers who have applied their learning to the principles of the Tao. It is important, however, to differentiate between those writers who truly understand the meaning and principles of Tao with all its wonders, and those who use the term simply as a vehicle for their own beliefs. Here, as always, we must apply one of the basic tenets of Taoist thought, that of clarity.

THOUGHTS AND IDEAS

It is not particularly difficult to find quotations from modern
day philosophers which express Taoist thought. Indeed,
it is an interesting exercise to listen to people around one and
truly 'hear' what they say. You may like to carry a notebook with
you and note down some of the following sayings so that you
can contemplate them at your leisure.

The idea of nothing has bugged people for centuries, especially in the
Western world. We have a saying in Latin, *Ex nihilo nuhil fit,* which
means "out of nothing comes nothing." It has occurred to me that
this is a fallacy of tremendous proportions. It lies at the root of all
our common sense, not only in the West, but in many parts of the
East as well. It manifests in a kind of terror of nothing, a put-down
on nothing, and a put-down on everything associated with nothing,
such as sleep, passivity, rest, and even the feminine principles. But to
me nothing – the negative, the empty – is exceedingly powerful. I
would say, on the contrary, you can't have something without
nothing. Image nothing but space, going on and on, with nothing in it
forever. But there you are imagining it, and you are something in it.
The whole idea of there being only space, and nothing else at all, is
not only inconceivable but perfectly meaningless, because we always
know what we mean by contrast.
Alan Watts

Chapter Three

And the whole idea is this, which you find reflected in the Taoist philosophy, that the moment you start interfering in the course of nature with a mind that is centered and one-pointed, and analyzes everything, and breaks it down into bits...The moment you do that you lost contact with your original know-how...by means of which you now colour your eyes, breathe, and beat your heart.

For thousands of years mankind has lost touch with his original intelligence, and he has been absolutely fascinated by this kind of political, godlike, controlling intelligence...where you can go ptt-ptt-ptt-ptt...and analyze things all over the place, and he has forgotten to trust his own organism.

Now the whole thing is that everything is coming to be realized today. Not only through people who take psychedelics, but also through many scientists. They're realizing that this linear kind of intelligence cannot keep up with the course of nature. It can only solve trivial problems when the big problems happen too fast to be thought about in that way. So, those of us who are in some way or other--through psychedelics, through meditation, through what have you--are getting back to being able to trust our original intelligence...are suggesting an entirely new course for the development of civilization.

Alan Ginsberg

The Houseboat Summit: February, 1967, Sausalito, California
Taken from *'The Oracle'* Issue no. 7

Along the Grain
The tao is nameless like uncarved wood

As soon as it is carved
Then there are names

Carve carefully
And
Along the Grain
Timothy Leary
Psychedelic Prayers

When you work with Wu Wei, you put the round peg in the round hole and the square peg in the square hole. No stress no struggle. Egotistical Desire tries to force the round peg into the square hole and vice-versa. Cleverness tries to devise craftier ways of making pegs fit where they don't belong. Knowledge tries to figure out why round pegs fit round holes, but not square holes. Wu Wei doesn't try. It doesn't think about it. It just does it. And when it does. It doesn't appear to do much if anything , But Things Get Done.
Benjamin Hoff
The Tao of Pooh

Always be peaceful and happy. Things are just as they are. Un- sagely people become renowned as sages and the true sages are often ignored. This is simply owning to the times and its character.

The Way bears sensation,
Sensation bears memory,
Sensation and memory bear abstraction,
And abstraction bears all the world;
Each thing in the world bears feeling and doing,
And, imbued with mind, harmony with the Way.

As others have taught, so do I teach,
"Who loses harmony opposes nature"
This is the root of my teaching.

Is the action of nature not unlike drawing a bow?
What is higher is pulled down, and what is lower is raised up;
What is taller is shortened, and what is thinner is broadened;
Nature's motion decreases those who have more than they need
And increases those who need more than they have.

It is not so with Man.
Man decreases those who need more than they have
And increases those who have more than they need.

To give away what you do not need is to follow the Way.
So the sage gives without expectation,
Accomplishes without claiming credit,
And has no desire for ostentation.

Chapter Four:

The Scriptures of Tao
and Taoism

Satisfied with his possessions,
the sage eliminates the need to steal;
at one with the Tao,
he remains free of envy,
and has no need of titles.

Though Lao Tse wrote the words himself – or rather expressed the sentiment in Chinese – he might have been talking of himself. The man who became known as Lao Tse had a given name which was Li Erh; the name Lao Tse means 'old sage' or 'old boy' and in that sense was simply an acknowledgement of his status. Lao Tse was a philosopher and probably the first person – though there are those who doubt as to whether he really existed – to record in writing his thoughts on the Tao.

Lao Tse is thought to have kept the Imperial Archives of the Court of Chou, in the province of Honan. According to legend, when Lao Tse was about to retire from public service he became disillusioned with Chinese society, mounted a horse and began riding west into the desert regions of China. Such behaviour, although it now seems romantic and full of meaning, would have been entirely natural in someone who was escaping from the world or seeking solitude. Before Lao Tse disappeared the border guard asked him to write down a synopsis of his teachings which he did over a period of two days in some five thousand characters. These writings became the *Tao Te Ching*.

In fact, there is some doubt as to whether or not he was the sole author of what has become one of the most widely read scriptures in the world. Some experts believe that more than one sage or 'old master' was involved, although ultimately it probably makes little difference. There are those who suggest that Confucius had visited him while others believe that this is a myth. Whatever happened, the legacy that was left behind is studied by many, right up to the present day.

It was believed for some time that few original copies of *Tao Te Ching* had survived, access to the scriptures being mainly through the received text of Wang Bi (AD 226–249) and Heshang Gong, a legendary figure depicted as a teacher to the Han Emperor Wen (179–157 BC). The discovery of two *Lao Tse* silk manuscripts at Mawangdui, near Changsha in the Hunan province in 1973 marked a surge forward in modern *Lao Tse* research. The tomb in which the manuscripts were found had been sealed in 168 BC so the texts had to predate that time. Students of the *Lao Tse* in the present day can work with several Chinese and Japanese studies that have made use of a large number of manuscript versions and stone inscriptions. As interest in China and things Chinese has grown, many people have offered translations of the *Lao Tse*, as the *Tao Te Ching* is sometimes known, and over the last few years many of these translations have become available over the Internet. Opinions vary as to whether the *Lao Tse* is a mystical document or a socio-political one. It is perhaps better to treat it as both and to accept that this is part of its charm. On a purely personal note, the choice seems to depend on what frame of mind one is in when one reads it as to which it seems to be.

The *Tao Te Ching* is not the sort of book that needs to be read from cover to cover in one sitting. It is divided into two main sections. The first part of the book is often called the *Tao Ching*: in thirty-seven chapters Lao Tse lays down his thoughts on the nameless formless entity known as Tao and what sort of person the individual needs to become. The second part of the text, chapter 38 to the end, is known as the *Te Ching* (the Book of Virtue). This division seems to be entirely arbitrary, Tao being the first word of the first section and

Virtue the first word of the second. It helps to have a little understanding of Chinese customs and culture in order to appreciate the *Tao Te Ching* in its entirety, but as a code of conduct for the ordinary mortal it is unsurpassed. Below, from the second chapter, are Lao Tse's suggestions for what attributes the wise man should possess:

Indeed the Wise Man's office
Is to work by being still;
He teaches not by speech
But by accomplishment;
He does for everything,
Neglecting none;
Their life he gives to all,
Possessing none;
And what he brings to pass
Depends on no one else.
As he succeeds,
He takes no credit
And just because he does not take it,
Credit never leaves him.

Some of the directives are incredibly simple while others are somewhat complex. We might compare the idea:

The Tao is called the Great Mother:
empty yet inexhaustible,
it gives birth to infinite worlds.

It is always present within you.
You can use it any way you want.

with the more complex:

Understanding harmony is called the Constant.
Knowing the Constant is called illumination.
Nourishing life is called blessing.
Having control of your breath is called strength.

As a focus for thought or a tool for meditation the *Tao Te Ching* can be used on a daily basis, but in keeping with the Tao it need not be used in any kind of a structured way. It can simply be opened at random and a passage chosen for contemplation. The interesting thing about this method is that the more you use it the more the passages appear to be relevant to your own situation: the more also you will find that your conduct conforms with the Tao. Eventually, rather than using the *Tao Te Ching* as a tool to discover how you should be acting, you will be using it as a reference book to ensure that you have acted appropriately. Finally you may come to know the texts so well that the appropriate text pops into your mind as you move through your everyday life.

The ideas that are presented can sometimes seem rather off-beam and yet at the same time pertinent. In chapter 20 particularly, the writer seems to acknowledge that he is different to his fellow men and yet if he has Tao he has nothing to fear. In another he says:

Being one with the Tao is to be at peace,
and to be in conflict with it,
leads to chaos and dysfunction.

Yet, apart from painting a broad picture, Lao Tse gives no particular direction as to how to achieve this peace. He advocates 'emptiness' and *wu wei* – doing nothing – and then leaves us to get on with it. We know from him what can be achieved but, unless we change our mind-set, not how to achieve it.

Lao Tse talks of rulers and princes and of how to govern the people, which is why the scriptures might be considered to be socio-political. However, it is only when his texts are read as though we ourselves are a country which is being ruled that we begin to understand. He is actually suggesting that this is how we can 'rule ourselves.' He says:

The sage follows the natural way,
doing what is required of him.

Like an experienced tracker,
he leaves no tracks;
like a good speaker, his speech is fluent;
He makes no error, so needs no tally;
like a good door, which needs no lock,
he is open when it is required of him,
and closed at other times;
like a good binding, he is secure,
without the need of borders.

Knowing that virtue may grow from example,
this is the way in which the sage teaches,
abandoning no one who stops to listen.
Thus, from experience of the sage,
all might learn, and so might gain.

There is mutual respect twixt teacher and pupil,
for, without respect, there would be confusion.

Shortly afterwards he says of the sage:

The sage has no invariable mind of his own; he makes the mind of
the people his mind.

To those who are good (to me), I am good; and to those who are not
good (to me), I am also good; and thus (all) get to be good. To those
who are sincere (with me), I am sincere; and to those who are not
sincere (with me), I am also sincere; and thus (all) get to be sincere.

The sage has in the world an appearance of indecision, and keeps his mind in a state of indifference to all. The people all keep their eyes and ears directed to him, and he deals with them all as his children.

And still later he muses, almost as though he is aware of how fickle the majority of people can be, of how much power can corrupt and how such rulers can be seduced by power.

If I were suddenly to become known, and (put into a position to) conduct (a government) according to the Great Tao, what I should be most afraid of would be a boastful display.

The great Tao (or way) is very level and easy; but people love the by-ways.

Their court (yards and buildings) shall be well kept, but their fields shall be ill-cultivated, and their granaries very empty. They shall wear elegant and ornamented robes, carry a sharp sword at their girdle, pamper themselves in eating and drinking, and have a super abundance of property and wealth; such (princes) may be called robbers and boasters. This is contrary to the Tao surely!

His feelings are quite clear as to how he knows such things to be true and how the wise man must act for he says:

A state may be ruled by (measures of) correction; weapons of war may be used with crafty dexterity; (but) the kingdom is made one's own (only) by freedom from action and purpose.

How do I know that it is so? By these facts: In the kingdom the multiplication of prohibitive enactments increases the poverty of the people; the more implements to add to their profit that the people have, the greater disorder is there in the state and clan; the more acts of crafty dexterity that men possess, the more do strange contrivances appear; the more display there is of legislation, the more thieves and robbers there are.

Therefore a sage has said, 'I will do nothing (of purpose), and the people will be transformed of themselves; I will be fond of keeping still, and the people will of themselves become correct. I will take no trouble about it, and the people will of themselves become rich; I will manifest no ambition, and the people will of themselves attain to the primitive simplicity.'

Sincere words are not fine; fine words are not sincere. Those who are skilled (in the Tâo) do not dispute (about it); the disputatious are not skilled in it. Those who know (the Tâo) are not extensively learned; the extensively learned do not know it.

The sage does not accumulate (for himself). The more that he expends for others, the more does he possess of his own; the more that he gives to others, the more does he have himself.

With all the sharpness of the Way of Heaven, it injures not; with all the doing in the way of the sage he does not strive.

Chuang Tse

We have seen previously how Chuang Tse proved an able follower of Lao Tse, but we also have to give credit to him for the power of his own scriptures. These are gathered under the title *Chuang Tse*, since Chinese books are given the name of their author. As usual with such ancient writings, there is doubt cast on the authenticity of all of the scriptures, most scholars believing that it is only the inner chapters that can be ascribed to Chuang Tse alone, many of the other chapters being a collection compiled by his pupils.

Of my sentences nine in ten are metaphorical; of my illustrations seven in ten are from valued writers. The rest of my words are like the water that daily fills the cup, tempered and harmonized by the Heavenly element in our nature.

Chapter Four

Chuang Tse takes Lao Tse's mystical viewpoints and shows how they are applicable to the ordinary everyday world. He does this without ever losing sight of their relevance to the sublime. He explains Virtue (*Tê*) as each individual's way of expressing Tao and thus makes the concept much more readily available and easily understandable. He also seems to be much more conscious of Nature and the individual's place within the system than Lao Tse. This leads him to recognize that self-transformation and self-responsibility are of prime importance. He says:

> The universe gives me my body so that I may be carried, my life so
> I may toil; my old age so I may repose, and my death so I may rest.
> To regard life as good is the way to regard death as good.

Chuang Tse is also aware that this self-transformation is only possible through the principle of Emptiness, that one must move through awareness of the senses. In one of his scriptures he writes as though Confucius were speaking to Yen Hui:

> *Yen Hui:*
> What is 'fasting of the heart?'
> *Confucius:*
> The goal of fasting is inner unity.
> This means hearing, but not with the ear;
> hearing, but not with the understanding;
> hearing with the spirit, with your whole being . . .
> The hearing of the spirit is not limited to any one faculty, to the ear, or to
> the mind.
> Hence it demands the emptiness of all the faculties.
> And when the faculties are empty, then the whole being listens.
> There is then a direct grasp of what is right there before you
> that can never be heard with the ear or understood with the mind.
> Fasting of the heart empties the faculties, frees you from limitation and
> from preoccupation.
> Fasting of the heart begets unity and freedom.

Yen Hui:
I see. What was standing in my way was my own self-awareness. If I can begin this fasting of the heart, self-awareness will vanish.

It can be seen that Chuang Tse concurs with the thoughts of Lao Tse in attempting to explain Tao when he says:

> Tao has reality and evidence but no action or physical form. It may be transmitted but cannot be received. It may be obtained but cannot be seen. It is based in itself, rooted in itself. Before Heaven and Earth came into being, Tao existed by itself for all time. It gave spirits and rulers their spiritual powers. It created Heaven and Earth. It is above the zenith but is not high. It is beneath the nadir but is not low. It is prior to Heaven and Earth but is not old. It is more ancient than the highest antiquity but is not regarded as long ago.

It must also be stressed that Chuang Tse's writings are largely philosophical and thus completely free from all of the aspects of magical practices that grew out of later scriptures, such as divinatory practices, the development of either external or internal alchemy and the search for an elixir of life. He attempts only to explain life in ways that we all can understand, to demonstrate by memorable or amusing anecdotes just what benefits a deep understanding of the processes of life bring the individual. Here he demonstrates true simplicity from the forces of Nature itself:

> Nan-kwo Tsze-khî was seated, leaning forward on his stool. He was looking up to heaven and breathed gently, seeming to be in a trance, and to have lost all consciousness of any companion. (His disciple), Yen Khang Tsze-yû, who was in attendance and standing before him, said, 'What is this? Can the body be made to become thus like a withered tree, and the mind to become like slaked lime? His appearance as he leans forward on the stool today is such as I never saw him have before in the same position.' Tsze-khî said,

'Yen, you do well to ask such a question, I had just now lost myself;
but how should you understand it? You may have heard the notes
of Man, but have not heard those of Earth; you may have heard the
notes of Earth, but have not heard those of Heaven.'

Tsze-yû said, 'I venture to ask from you a description of all
these.' The reply was, 'When the breath of the Great Mass (of
nature) comes strongly, it is called Wind. Sometimes it does not
come so; but when it does, then from a myriad apertures there
issues its excited noise; have you not heard it in a prolonged gale?
Take the projecting bluff of a mountain forest; in the great trees, a
hundred spans round, the apertures and cavities are like the
nostrils, or the mouth, or the ears; now square, now round like a
cup or a mortar; here like a wet footprint, and there like a large
puddle. (The sounds issuing from them are like) those of fretted
water, of the arrowy whizz, of the stern command, of the inhaling
of the breath, of the shout, of the gruff note, of the deep wail, of
the sad and piping note. The first notes are slight, and those that
follow deeper, but in harmony with them. Gentle winds produce a
small response; violent winds a great one. When the fierce gusts
have passed away, all the apertures are empty (and still); have you
not seen this in the bending and quivering of the branches and
leaves?'

Tsze-yû said, 'The notes of Earth then are simply those which
come from its myriad apertures; and the notes of Man may just be
compared to those which (are brought from the tubes of) bamboo;
allow me to ask about the notes of Heaven.' Tsze-khî replied,
'When (the wind) blows, (the sounds from) the myriad apertures
are different, and (its cessation) makes them stop of themselves.
Both of these things arise from (the wind and the apertures)
themselves: should there be any other agency that excites them?'

Neither is Chuang Tse above using the ordinary and the idiosyncrasies of life
to illustrate a point. He says of one he calls Cripple Shu:

Consider Cripple Shu. His chin is down by his navel. His shoulders
stick up above his head. The bones at the base of his neck point to
the sky. The five pipes of his spine are on top: his two thighs form
ribs. Yet by sewing and washing he is able to fill his mouth; by
shaking the fortune-telling sticks he earns enough to feed ten.
When the authorities draft soldiers, a cripple can walk among them
confidently flapping his sleeves; when they are conscripting work
gangs, cripples are excused because of their infirmity. When the
authorities give relief grain to the ailing a cripple gets three
measures along with bundles of firewood. Thus one whose form is
crippled can nurture his body and live out the years Heaven grants
him. Think what he may do if his virtue was crippled too!

However he also states very clearly the three aspects of awareness which
constitute man in his perfection – the ideal to which we all aspire. He states:

Not to be separate from his primal source constitutes what we call
the Heavenly man; not to be separate from the essential nature
thereof constitutes what we call the Spirit-like man; not to be
separate from its real truth constitutes what we call the Perfect
man.

Lieh Tse

Lieh Tse, sometimes known as the third founder of Taoism, slightly predates
Chuang Tse and probably achieved immortality, or at least magical powers,
since there is a script which states that he was perceived by Chuang Tse flying
through the air. The writings attributed to him use stories and fables and
illustrate some of the magical powers of the ancient sages who were so 'in the
Tao' that they were able to prolong life, walk through solid rock and levitate.

In common with the other scriptures there are those who think it unlikely
that there was a single author for these writings, it being more than likely that
they were a collection of stories put together as Taoism began to become

popular. There are others who believe that Lieh Tse is simply another 'version' or aspect of Lao Tse. Not everything has survived but, like the other scriptures, these writings also are very clear-sighted about the various functions of the parts of the cosmos and, using the same concepts as Chuang Tse, describe them in this way:

> The Master Lieh Tse said: 'The virtue of Heaven and Earth, the powers of the Sage, and the uses of the myriad things in Creation, are not perfect in every direction. It is Heaven's function to produce life and to spread a canopy over it. It is Earth's function to form material bodies and to support them. It is the Sage's function to teach others and to influence them for good. It is the function of created things to conform to their proper nature. That being so, there are things in which Earth may excel, though they lie outside the scope of Heaven; matters in which the Sage has no concern, though they afford free play to others. For it is clear that that which imparts and broods over life cannot form and support material bodies; that which forms and supports material bodies cannot teach and influence for good; one who teaches and influences for good cannot run counter to natural instincts; that which is fixed in suitable environment does not travel outside its own sphere. Therefore the Way of Heaven and Earth will be either of the Yin or of the Yang; the teaching of the Sage will be either of altruism or of righteousness; the quality of created objects will be either soft or hard. All these conform to their proper nature and cannot depart from the province assigned to them.'

Lieh Tse denies any difference between the spirit and the body and, therefore, the existence of any transcendent state outside of matter and its animating *chi* (essential energy). For him the only difference between the spirit and the body is represented by their different grades of *chi*:

> The spiritual element in man is allotted to him by Heaven, his

corporeal frame by Earth. The part that belongs to Heaven is ethereal and dispersive, the part that belongs to Earth is dense and tending to conglomeration. When the spirit parts from the body, each of these elements returns to its proper place. That is why disembodied spirits are called *kuei*, which means 'returning', that is, returning to their true dwelling place.

To demonstrate his attitude to life and death we find the following:

Lieh Tse left his home in Cheng and journeyed to the kingdom of Wei. While walking down a dusty road, he saw the remains of a skull lying by the wayside. Lieh Tse saw that it was the skull of a human that was over a hundred years old. He picked up the bone, brushed the dirt off it, and looked at it for a while. Finally, he put the skull down, sighed, and said to his student who was standing nearby, 'In this world, only you and I understand life and death.' Turning to the skull he said, 'Are you unfortunate to be dead and are we fortunate to be alive? Maybe it is you who are fortunate and we who are unfortunate!'

Lieh Tse then said to his student, 'Many people sweat and toil and feel satisfied that they have accomplished many things. However, in the end we are not all that different from this polished piece of bone. In a hundred years, everyone we know will be just a pile of bones. What is there to gain in life, and what is there to lose in death?'

The ancients knew that life cannot go on forever, and death is not the end of everything. Therefore, they are not excited by the event of life nor depressed by the occurrence of death. Birth and death are part of the natural cycle of things. Only those who can see through the illusion of life and death can be renewed with heaven and earth and age with the sun, moon, and stars.

Hua hu Ching

One final scripture which has only recently been brought to notice is the *Hua hu Ching*. It is said to be constructed from the oral teachings of Lao Tse and the translator states:

> The teachings of the Hua Hu Ching are of enormous power and consequence, a literal road map to the divine realm for ordinary human beings. Perhaps predictably, the book was banned during a period of political discord in China, and all copies were ordered to be burned. Were it not for the Taoist tradition of oral transmission of sacred scriptures from master to student, they would have been lost forever. I am permanently indebted to Taoist Master Ni Hua-Ching for sharing his version of these teachings with the Western world after his emigration from China in 1976.

There seems to be no mention of this scripture in the *Tao Tsang* and the consensus of opinion is that it is probably not genuine. It is from the fourth century, possibly later, and it may or may not be a forgery; there is not enough evidence to form an opinion either way.

This is a good illustration of how it can be quite difficult to differentiate between what is genuine and what is not when studying Tao. For many people it is enough to begin with the *Tao Te Ching*, then follow their intuition as to the next steps to be taken. We can do no more in this book than trace the history of the religious scriptures as they were gathered together over the years. If you are of an inquisitive frame of mind then the scriptures which belong to the *Tao Tsang* (Taoist Canon) will offer food for thought.

The Tao Tsang

The *Tao Tsang* follows on from the early scriptures of the *Tao Te Ching* and Chuang Tse and is the Taoist Canon (body of writings) which has been developed over many centuries. There were 1,120 diverse items of information available in the late fifth century and the first *Tao Tsang* was put together as a single comprehensive catalogue. It was assembled on the orders of Sung Ming-ti by Lu Hsui-Ching. It consisted of scriptures, pharmaceutical works, talismans and diagrams which were concerned with enabling the ascent of the soul to heaven – a major concern in all later Taoist writings. (This is of interest since, as we have seen, the earlier writings were more concerned with understanding how to live in harmony with the forces of Nature.)

The *Lingpo* sect therefore acquired a distinctive liturgy since Lu Hsiu-Ching arranged the diverse Taoist texts into three groups. These were probably based upon the model of the Buddhist *Tipitaka* (Three Baskets). Taoist writings generally were classified according to the three Caverns or Grottoes (*san tung*) and belong to three revelatory traditions:

- The *Tung-Chen* section (Pervasive Perfection) evolved around the Supreme Clarity scriptures.
- The *Tung-Hsuan* (Pervasive Mystery) evolved around the Scriptures of Numinous Treasures.
- The *Tung-Shen* (Pervasive Divinity) evolved around the Scriptures of Three Sovereigns or Kings.

There were twelve further subdivisions of the Grottoes which were as follows:

1. Original revelations
2. Divine talismans
3. Interpretations
4. Sacred diagrams
5. Histories and genealogies
6. Codes of conduct
7. Ceremonial protocols
8. Prescriptive rituals
9. Special techniques (alchemical, geomantic and numerological)
10. Sacred writings
11. Songs of Praise
12. Memorial Communications

From then on, the various canons were given specific names. In the early twelfth century, Sung Hui-Tsang initiated an ambitious programme which resulted in the *Cheng-ho Wan-Shou Tao Tsang* (the Taoist Canon of the Longevity of the *Cheng-ho*). This Canon, prepared on wooden blocks, was the first to be printed. In 1210 the *Ta Chin Hsuan-Tu Pao Tsang* (Precious Canon of the Arcane Metropolis of the Great Chin) totalled over 6,400 *Chuan* or scriptures. The Canon most in use today is based on a compilation completed between 1444 and 1445 and supplemented in 1607.

Immortality

A large percentage of the Taoist Canon deals with the subject of long life or immortality. Most of these writings are very obscure – partly because of difficulties with translation – and are often decipherable only to those who have been initiated into their mysteries. They are perhaps becoming more available to the Western thinker nowadays as disciplines from the East such as *Tai Chi*, *Chi Gung*, and other practices which have their roots in Tao, are adopted in the West. The particularly Chinese qualities of patience, egotism (self-understanding), reserve, contentment and tranquillity are all there to be understood and adopted, although the writings often use a hidden, multi-level, symbolic language.

The *Tao Te Ching* itself is considered by some to have been a code of behaviour for young initiates, rather than one man's philosophical treatise. The *Hsiang-erh-Chu* commentary is the only substantial writing associated with the early Masters that has survived; it prescribes rules of conduct and techniques of meditative practice. Many of the later writings were given the addition of alchemical terms.

There were practices which were designed to aid in the restoration of world order and in the attainment of immortality for the individual. The need for entry into the divine ranks called for an extensive body of literature. Much of the *Tao Tsang* explains, in plain language, breath control practices which are designed to prolong life through the taking in of subtle energies. It was believed that by gaining control over the vital forces of the sun, moon and stars and being able to absorb these sources of radiance, the individual could achieve 'cosmic transmigration.'

It is not known where exactly these teachings began – the *Tao Te Ching* of Lao Tse states that 'the epitome of virtue is to obtain immortality' – but they did become part of the *Shangqing* (also *Shang Ch'ing*) school's revelations in the fourth century. This school was dominated by adepts who recognized the influences of wind and water (*Feng Shui*) on the world in which they lived. The *Lingpao* scriptural tradition also accepted the principle of astral energy.

Rituals

Many of the rituals still in use today had their beginning in the *Lingpao* traditions, which owe a great deal both to the arcana of southern Chinese religious practice and to Mahayana Buddhism. The protocols were largely laid down by Tu Kuang-t'ing in the late ninth and early tenth centuries. For instance, the practice of inscribing propitiatory prayers on metal, wood or golden dragons and casting them into caves or streams – known as the 'casting dragons' ritual – was done to ensure the safety of the kingdom. This rite has close ties with the Roman ritual of using 'curse tablets' to focus one's ill feeling over real or imagined wrongs. Many present-day pagans use a similar sort of ritual to rid themselves of negativity.

One of the most important festivals of religious Taoism, known since its beginnings, is *chai*. In the official state ritual, *chai* designates a fast before sacrifices, a way of cleansing oneself of harmful influences. In Taoism the term refers to feasts held under the direction of a master, at which a specific number of pupils (between six and 38) participate. These feasts serve mainly for the confessions of sins, which are considered to be the cause of all illness.

Chai ceremonies are very complicated and those participating at them require detailed instruction. They are usually held in the courtyard of Taoist monasteries and may extend over several days. Every school of religious Taoism celebrates its own fasts. These are particularly important in the *T'ai-P'ing Tao*, *Wu-Tou-Mi Tao* and the *Ling-Pao p'ai* schools.

One of the best known ceremonies is the *t'u-t'an chai* – a fast during which the participants smear themselves with charcoal. After a platform of strictly prescribed dimensions – its sides limited by ropes – has been erected, the participants, holding hands, step onto it. Their hair is tangled and their faces are covered with coal dust and dirt to signify their remorse. To the accompaniment of a drum, the master of the ceremony implores various deities to attend the feast. There follows a recitation of sins and their possible consequences. At this point the religious ecstasy of the participants reaches its peak. They throw themselves to the ground and roll in the dust to demonstrate their repentance.

As twelve vows of repentance are recited, the participants touch their foreheads to the ground and ask for their sins to be forgiven. The ceremony ends with further rituals. These collective repentance sessions are held three times daily, but the participants are only allowed to eat one meal a day. The resultant physical exhaustion produces a psychic collapse, which effects an inner purification.

Sacred Space

The concept of sacred space is another subject treated at length in the *Tao Tsang*. The *wu yueh* (sacred mountains, also known as the Five Peaks) were:

> *T'ai Shan,* Taoist mountain of the east, Shantung province
> *Heng Shan Bei,* Taoist mountain of the north, Shanxi province
> *Hua Shan,* Taoist mountain of the west, Shanxi province
> *Heng Shan Nan,* Taoist mountain of the south, Hunan province
> *Song Shan,* Taoist mountain of the centre, Henan province

The best known of the Five Peaks was *T'ai Shan* (opposite). It was said that it was here that seventy-two sovereigns of antiquity performed the *feng* sacrifice in which they announced to Heaven the complete success of their government. This ritual, which seems to have had a profound effect on later Taoist scripture, was designed by the *fang-shih* magicians for the First Emperor (Ch'in Shih-huang-ti) and for Emperor Wu of the Han dynasty (c.

140–87 BC). According to popular belief, it was held that the dead went to live on T'ai Shan, since the god who resided there was lord over the fate of humans; he kept a 'life reckoning' for each person. Only later did the god of T'ai Shan become more devilish in his attributes.

These five mountains were not, however, the only – or even the most important – of the Taoist sacred peaks, and it is worthwhile understanding the relevance of mountains and grottoes in Taoism.

In the Taoist religion, the Grotto Heavens and Blissful Realms are classified into the Ten Great Grotto Heavens, the Thirty-Six Lesser Grotto Heavens, and the Seventy-Two Blissful Realms. These are places on earth which the Immortals and deities inhabit in order to cultivate Tao and attain immortality; they are places which are found in famous mountains and cave dwellings. (We have already seen that the symbols of grottoes are used in the classification of the scriptures.) To penetrate into the mountains, the Taoists had to use prestigious talismans, in particular the *Wu yueh chen-hsing t'u* (Diagram of the Real Form of the Five Peaks) and other sets of 'five talismans'.

While recognizing this identification of the Five Peaks with Taoism and their possible further link with the Five Elements, it is fair to say that the mountains already had achieved a sanctity of their own. They were worshipped as a part of nature and as guardians of magic by the Taoists' shamanic predecessors long before Taoism had taken on an organized religious form. It is only from the late sixth century onwards that Taoists made a real effort to claim these particular mountains as their own although they were never totally successful in establishing their claim. More important to Taoist history, mountains such as Mao Shan and Lung-hu Shan were centres, respectively, of *Shangqing* and *Cheng-i* Taoism. Together with *Ko-tsao Shan* (in Chiangsi), the ordination centre of *Lingpao* Taoism, these mountains and holy places constituted the spiritual centres for Taoism as it developed after the twelfth century. Many are still in use today.

There is a rich source of information on the beliefs and practices of the Taoist masters in their collected writings should one wish to pursue that line of research. Many of the disciples of these masters ensured that their words were preserved for posterity. One such lyrical piece is the *Pu-hsu tzu* (Lyrics on Pacing the Void) by Wu Yun, an ordained Cheng-i master.

THOUGHTS AND IDEAS

I have no reasons for choosing the quotations in this chapter other
than that they express for me the basic ethos behind the Tao.
By now, I would strongly advise you to have got, begged,
borrowed or stolen – well perhaps not – your own copy of
Tao te Ching at least. You should be able to use it as a quick
reference point in all sorts of situations. Open it when you are on
a train or a bus and simply begin reading. You will learn something.
When you can't think what your next action should be,
just read a portion. When you are ready find some of the other
scriptures either on the Internet or your local bookstore.

Deep Significance of the Spring and Autumn Annals
If we examine these wonders and portents carefully, we may discern
the will of Heaven. The will of Heaven desires us to do certain
things and not to do others. As to those things which Heaven wishes
and does not wish, if a man searches within himself, he will surely
find warnings of them in his own heart, and if he looks about him at
daily affairs, he will find verification of these warnings in the state.
Thus we can discern the will of Heaven in these portents and
wonders. We should not hate such signs, but stand in awe of them,
considering that Heaven wishes to repair our faults and save us from
our errors. Therefore it takes this way to warn us.
Tung Chung-shu, 'Ch'un-ch'iu fan-lu'

Hui Tzu said to Chuang Tzu, "The king of Wei gave me some seeds
of a huge gourd. I planted them, and when they grew up, the fruit
was big enough to hold five piculs. I tried using it for a water
container, but it was so heavy I couldn't lift it. I split it in half to make
dippers, but they were so large and unwieldly that I couldn't dip
them into anything. It's not that the gourds weren't fantastically big –
but I decided they were no use and so I smashed them to pieces."

Chuang Tzu said, "You certainly are dense when it comes to using
big things! In Sung there was a man who was skilled at making a salve
to prevent chapped hands, and generation after generation his family
made a living by bleaching silk in water. A traveller heard about the
salve and offered to buy the prescription for a hundred measures of
gold. The man called everyone to a family council. 'For generations
we've been bleaching silk and we've never made more than a few
measures of gold,' he said. 'Now, if we sell our secret, we can make
a hundred measures in one morning. Let's let him have it!'

The traveller got the salve and introduced it to the king of Wu, who
was having trouble with the state of Yüeh. The king put the man in
charge of his troops, and that winter they fought a naval battle with
the men of Yüeh and gave them a bad beating. A portion of the
conquered territory was awarded to the man as a fief. The salve had
the power to prevent chapped hands in either case; but one made
used it to get a fief, while the other one never got beyond silk
bleaching – because they used it in different ways. Now you had a
gourd big enough to hold five piculs. Why didn't you think of making
it into a great tub so you could go floating around the rivers and
lakes, instead of worrying because it was too big and unwieldy to dip
into things! Obviously you still have a lot of underbrush in your head!"

Chuang Tse in 'Spiritual Teachings of the Tao' by Mark Forstater

How can the divine Oneness be seen?
In beautiful forms, breathtaking wonders, awe-inspiring miracles?
The Tao is not obliged to present itself in this way.
If you are willing to be lived by it, you will see it
everywhere, even in the most ordinary things.
Hua Hu Ching

Use fairness in governing the state.
Use surprise tactics in war.
Be unconcerned and you will have the world.
How do I know it is like this?
Because:
The more regulations there are,
The poorer people become.
The more people own lethal weapons,
The more darkened are the country and clans.
The more clever the people are,
The more extraordinary actions they take.
The more picky the laws are,
The more thieves and gangsters there are.
Therefore the sages say:
"I do not force my way and the people transform themselves.
I enjoy my serenity and the people correct themselves.
I do not interfere and the people enrich themselves."

Tell a man that he is merely following the opinions of another, or
that he is a flatterer of others, and at once he flushes with anger.
And yet all his life he is merely following others, and is flattering
them! His illustrations are made to agree with theirs, his phrases
are glossed – to win the approbation of the multitudes. From first
to last, from beginning to end, he finds no fault with their views.
He dresses so as to win the favour of his age, and yet does not
call himself a flatterer. He is but a follower of those others,
approving or disapproving as they do, and yet he will not say that
he is one of them. This is the height of stupidity.

Don't nourish a bird as you would nourish yourself - you will
make them perplexed and frightened. He who would nourish a
bird as a bird should be nourished should let it perch in a deep
forest, or let it float on a river or lake, or let it find its food
naturally and undisturbed on the level dry ground.

To him who does not dwell in himself the forms of things show
themselves as they are. His movement is like that of water
(flowing), his stillness is like that of a mirror (showing things just
as they are). His tenuity makes him seem to be disappearing
altogether; he is still as a clear lake, harmonious in his association
with others, and he counts gain as loss. Men all prefer to be first,
he alone chooses to be last. Men all choose fullness, he alone
chooses emptiness. He does not store, and therefore he has a
superabundance; he looks solitary, but has a multitude around
him. In his conducting himself he is easy and leisurely and wastes
nothing. He does nothing, and laughs at the clever and ingenious.

Chapter Five:

Tao and Other Beliefs

Over many millennia people have developed faith in an ultimate force or power, which they have expressed in many different ways. On the face of it, these faiths seem to be essentially different to one another. However, when they are investigated more closely, it becomes obvious that there are a number of outstanding similarities. For instance, there is a distinct relationship between the various traditions of the Middle East and Asia. Buddhism, Hinduism and Confucianism all have very similar philosophies and practices although they all appear to have different origins or concepts. We look first at the Hindu faith, purely and simply because it is one of the best-known of the Eastern religions.

Hinduism

Within the Hindu faith the way to finding Ultimate Truth is through releasing oneself from the need for material possessions and pleasures. This is called *Moksha* which means 'freedom'. More precisely, *Moksha* means freedom from the cycle of birth and rebirth. It is achievable by recognizing that *Samsara* – reincarnation based on past actions – is unnecessary when one comes to the realization that the material world is one of illusion and fragmentation.

Yoga, which means 'union with the divine,' is the discipline through which human potential can be released and *Samadhi* (absorption in the Divine) achieved. The various forms of yoga relate to the specific direction that the individual follows in order to unleash the power of *Moksha*. The *Bhagavad Gita* – probably the best-known scripture – mentions three major yoga systems. These are:

Karma Yoga, yoga of action, which aims to help the practitioner to evolve spiritually by selflessly serving and assisting others.

Bhakti Yoga, the yoga of devotion, which requires devotion to the divine and all its manifestations.

Jnana Yoga, the yoga of knowledge, which leads to philosophical discrimination by which jnana, or the knowledge of Brahman (the Supreme Reality), is attained.

There are also at least two other major Yoga systems:

Raja Yoga, the yoga of mind control, which achieves its purpose mainly through meditation and spiritual purification.

Hatha Yoga, the yoga of physical exercise and breath control, which helps the practitioner to bring the inner being into line with the spiritual self, through the use of asanas or postures.

There is a group of techniques (called the Eight Limbs of Yoga), common to all systems of yoga, which are perceived as being steps along the journey of exploration that results in the self-discipline necessary for union with the Divine. They are:

1. *Yama:* The essence of Yama is not to harm any living creature in either thought, word or deed and indicates the application

of restraint and self-control. Yama embodies the principles of non-violence (ahimsa), truthfulness (satya), non-stealing (asteya), chastity or sexual abstinence (brahmacarya) and freedom from materialism (aparigraha).

2. *Niyama:* *Niyama* establish order in everyday life and are personal disciplines to be observed. These are cleanliness of mind and body *(sauca),* contentment *(santosa),* commitment *(tapas),* introspective study *(svadhyaya)* and surrender of all thoughts and actions to the Ultimate *(Isvarapranidhana).*

3. *Asanas:* These are the yoga postures which allow body and mind to move in harmony and eventually to become absorbed within the infinite. *Asanas* are described as creating steadiness *(sthira)* and joyfulness *(sukham).* Confusion thus disappears.

4. *Pranayama:* This is breath control and the art of Yoga breathing. *Prana* (life-breath) is the link between each individual entity and the cosmos and is similar to chi in Chinese thought. *Pranayama* consists of regulation and refinement of the inhalation, exhalation and retention of breath and leads to an inward focus giving access to Universal Truth.

5. *Pratyhara:* This is the further withdrawal of the senses from the external world. Outward trivialities cease to intrude on one's contemplation of the inner world.

6. *Dharana:* This is focussed concentration on a point, object or concept without distraction.

7. *Dhyana:* This is true meditation. The object or concept that one is contemplating becomes all absorbing and the mind

achieves a degree of concentration which enables conscious understanding to develop.

8. *Samadhi:* This is a state of bliss and union with the Divine which transcends meditation. Consciousness becomes absorbed in a state of peace and tranquility which gives one access through the soul to the Ultimate.

For the Hindu there are at least three paths to the Ultimate or union with the Divine. He believes that the first way is through knowledge. The three steps taken on this particular path are learning, thinking and – perhaps a little more complex – separating one's material ego from one's *Atman* (supreme spiritual principle).

The second way to the Ultimate is through love. Here, the love we show to others in, for instance, service and compassion can be translated into a love for God. One aspect of this love is through the work that we do. Through devotion to one's life task it is possible to perceive the power of a greater force at work in the world.

The final Hindu path to God is through exercises that form a link between the physical body and the psyche (spirit). In this way, the Hindu experiments with mental exercises and observes their effects on his material world. Not all Hindus take the same path to God, but the goal is identical.

Buddhism

Buddhism was established by Siddhartha Gautama, a prince of the Sakya kingdom who was a contemporary of Confucius. He became the Buddha or 'enlightened one' and brought about a great deal of reform in the consideration of the Ultimate.

He called the way between sensuality and asceticism the Middle Path, seeing Buddhism as a natural religion. There is no finality or rest within the universe, only a ceaseless becoming and never-ending change. All forms of life, according to the Buddha, can be shown to have three characteristics in common; impermanence, suffering, and an absence of an immortal soul – Man is always changing and is entirely mortal.

Buddha postulated that human beings are born and die according to their self-created Karma. This means that every action we perform leaves an impression on our very subtle mind, and each karmic potential eventually gives rise to its own effect. Positive or virtuous actions sow the seeds of future happiness, and negative or non-virtuous actions sow the seeds of future suffering. With a deeper understanding of the concept, we come to realize that the laws of Karma require that we harm nothing – neither the mind, nor the body of man nor any living thing. There are four aspects of Karma which are:

1. Cause and Effect

2. Compensation

3. Balancing

4. Completion

Although several different forms of Buddhism have come into existence since Buddha's death, there is a set of basic beliefs called the four Noble Truths that all Buddhists agree with and recognize. To Kadampa Buddhists – a branch of Mahayana Buddhism that later integrated with Taoism – all things are totally empty of any defining essence, similar to the no-thing of Taoism.

1. The first Noble Truth of the world according to Buddha is *Dhukka*, or the existence of impermanence. This might be defined as the recognition that all life suffers – this suffering may be physical or mental. To experience suffering is to come to terms with life on the lower planes of existence and appreciate just how impermanent those levels are.

2. The second Noble Truth is the cause of suffering – *Samudayha*. Buddha discovered that the direct causes of suffering are desire (tanha*) or craving, and* ignorance. Coming to terms with your desires and cravings means that you can eventually overcome them, but this cannot be done until you have knowledge.

3. The third Noble Truth is that in order to free yourself from suffering, you must overcome desire. This is *Nirohda*. To end suffering completely you must remove desire, ill will and ignorance. The end of suffering has been described as supreme happiness and Enlightenment. However, these terms do not fully express the real nature of the end of suffering, or *Nirvana*. As with Tao, *Nirvana* cannot be exactly put into words.

4. The fourth Noble Truth is that of the path leading to the end of suffering – *Magga*. Those who follow the Middle Path and avoid the extremes of indulging in their desires or of unreasonably torturing their bodies and minds will find happiness, peace of mind and what is now called Enlightenment. 'Enlightenment' is not the literal translation of any classical Buddhist term, however, but an attempt to describe the state of being. There is always plenty of light imagery in Buddhism, especially in *Mahayana* which is the form which lent itself to Taoism. Knowledge, understanding and intellect bring about clarity.

According to Buddha, the Eightfold Path is the chief way in which we can achieve freedom from suffering. Specifically, this path embodies:

1. *Right Understanding*: This is the understanding of the Four Noble Truths as a whole. One of the factors that constitute wisdom, this type of understanding knows the true nature of all things on a very deep level.

2. *Right Thought*: This is another of the factors that constitute wisdom. The Qualities of selfless renunciation, objectivity, love and non-violence are extended to all beings. Where selfish desire, hatred and violence prevail, people are lacking in integrity.

3. *Right Speech*: This is the way to ethical conduct. Truth, honesty and lack of malice are appropriate as ways of achieving harmony with others. Hasty words are unnecessary. Speaking carefully and appropriately is to be encouraged.

4. *Right Action*: This means acting with awareness and careful thought. By acting within the norms of the society in which one lives, one preserves the qualities of integrity and correctness. Ethical conduct is rooted in Right Action.

5. *Right Livelihood*: This constitutes living according to the four Noble Truths to the best of your ability. There can be no compromising in day-to-day living, and it is considered wrong to profit from the misfortune of others.

6. *Right Effort*: This is a mental discipline which requires that one is continuously vigilant in preventing evil and states of confusion in others. By creating an environment of tranquillity you are capable of promoting good and harmonious states of mind in others.

7. *Right Mindfulness*: This is another mental discipline which requires one to be fully conscious of the physical, emotional and spiritual state. You should attempt to be fully detached from these things, merely noticing them as they happen. It is important not to get caught up in fantasy and illusion.

8. *Right Concentration*: This is a discipline which allows you to use meditation and other such techniques to keep the mind under control. By focusing correctly the individual is enabled to slow the whirl of non-stop thought and bring about a calm and clear state of being.

Simply put, Buddha advocated the eradication of suffering, egoism and hatred. In this way, the novitiate could achieve *Nirvana*, a state of bliss in which there is complete non-attachment. The achievement of liberation then for the Buddhist occurs in *Nirvana*, when people release their yearning for a false selfhood. This of course is similar to Hindu belief and the search for

Samadhi. As with Hinduism, the act of getting rid of this yearning occurs simultaneously with a change of awareness or consciousness which has been called Enlightenment. This however is not a 'thing' to be found but a state of being to which one aspires.

The most challenging concept in Buddhism for the Hindus to accept was that Buddha taught that there was no such thing as the individual soul. Hindus thought that the *Atman*, or soul, was actually God, but Buddha reasoned that if the soul is purely God, then it is not individual and therefore is *An-Atman*, or 'no soul'. Every thing that exists has no fixed identity ('inherent existence') and therefore is in a state of impermanence – change and flux – constantly developing and decaying. This concept is similar to that of the cycles of change as we see them today in the Book of Changes (*I Ching*) in Chinese thought and in Taoism.

Confucianism

Another religion which one can relate to Hinduism and Buddhism is Confucianism. There is a great deal to admire in this religion. It has instigated a tremendously high standard of morality, being based on ethical conduct, and has taught a very clear concept of the 'Supreme Heaven God'. It led to the refinement of literary education and good conduct, similar to the Right Action of the Buddhists. While it was the State religion of China, Confucianism had a profound influence on the lives of the people.

The ethical teachings that were laid down as being important include the following values:

1. *Li:* This concerns propriety, etiquette and the use of ritual. The ideal way to operate, it gives order to all human relationships and results in a model social structure and harmonious living. The understanding of Heaven and Earth, ancestors, sovereigns and teachers all give rise to the hierarchical structure which permits appreciation and worship in the correct form.

2. *Hsiao:* This is love within the family structure and the respect of parents for their children and of children for their parents. The reverence due from son to parents means that he must contribute to their comfort and bring happiness and honour to their name by being successful in his own right.

3. *Yi:* Righteousness (abiding within the laws of Man and Nature) develops the consciousness as to the correct relationship between human beings. Impartiality, acting appropriately, respect and tolerance all lead to an upright and selfless personality. Righteousness should be superior to material profit and justice should stand above ownership.

4. *Xin:* Honesty and trustworthiness are a prime necessity in life's transactions. This requires the individual to be truthful and straightforward in speech, faithful to their promises and conscientious in dealings with others. *Yi* and *Xin* combined are similar to Right Action in Buddhism.

5. *Jen:* The highest Confucian virtue is benevolence and a humane attitude towards others, particularly within the community in which one lives. Awareness of others' needs and a willingness to help in times of difficulty allows the individual to express *Jen* as service to others.

6. *Chung:* This represents loyalty to the state, or rather, service to the wider world as represented by authority. Since emperors and rulers were seen to have ultimate authority over their people, this also implies that any higher authority (e.g. God) must be obeyed in this context.

The principle known as the 'Golden Rule' in the West – do as you would be done by – leads to a system of fundamental relationships which form the basis of Confucian social order. Developed from the philosophy of the *I Ching*, correct interrelationships within the dynamics of the family lay down the basis for the whole natural order of civilization. Actually, this order is based upon the relationships as laid out in the *Pa Kua* seen in Chapter 6.

However, before the development of Confucianism as a religion, Lao Tse had highlighted the idea of correct order in the *Tao Te Ching* and had spoken of the right conduct of emperors and rulers. It is believed by some that Confucius and Lao Tse met at one stage on their separate journeys towards the Truth, and of course both would have had access to earlier philosophical thought and scriptures. The difference between Confucianism and Taoism is that Confucianism perceives order from a human ethical standpoint, whereas Taoism works from a philosophical, naturalistic perspective.

Confucius believed that it was possible to revive the Chinese culture by returning to ancient values and redefining the importance of society and government. He described a society governed by reasonable, humane and correct discernment, not by the actions of those empowered solely by hereditary status. This could be achieved through education and the unification of cultural beliefs. The nation would benefit from a people who were culturally aware and who had been consciously educated by those aware of the consequences of such an education. Rituals and magic, rather than being tools of power, were something to be shared by the community as a mark of respect. It is unfortunate that the very attributes of a society that was designed to prevent manipulation later became tools for manipulating society.

Since the time of the Han dynasty (AD 206) there have been four rites of passage that have been recognized and regulated by Confucian tradition:

1. Birth

The *T'ai-shen* (spirit of the foetus) is thought to protect the pregnant woman and causes difficulty for anyone who upsets the mother-to-be. Special rites are carried out when the placenta is disposed of after birth. At this time the mother is given a special diet and then allowed rest for a month. The mother's nuclear family supplies all the baby's requirements on the first, fourth and twelfth monthly anniversary of the birth, thus demonstrating respect.

2. Reaching maturity

Except in particularly traditional families, this life passage is no longer considered to have much importance. Where it is celebrated, a special meal is presented for the whole family in which chicken is served to the young adult.

3. Marriage (This is performed in six stages)

Proposal

The couple exchange the eight characters of their natal astrology (representations of the year, month, day and hour of each of their births). If any unfortunate event occurs within the bride-to-be's family during the next three days, the proposal is either deemed to have been rejected or to have gone against correct action.

Engagement

After the wedding day is chosen, the bride announces the wedding with invitations and a gift of moon-shaped biscuits, thus honouring the feminine principle (*yin*).

Dowry

Both families treat one another with considerable respect. This is done in the following way: the bride's dowry is carried to the groom's home in a solemn procession; the groom's parents then return the compliment by sending the bride-price to her; gifts by the groom to the bride, equal in value to the dowry, are also sent.

Procession

The groom visits the bride's home and invites her to return with him to his own home. This is done with much ceremony.

Marriage and Reception

The couple recite their vows, toast each other with wine and then attend a lavish banquet in their honour.

Following Morning

As a mark of respect and to honour her new status in the family, the bride serves breakfast to the groom's parents, who then reciprocate.

4. Death

When death occurs, the neighbours are informed by hearing the cries of mourning. At this point, sorrow is indicated by the family putting on clothes made of coarse material. The corpse is then washed and placed in its coffin. The community helps the family mourners by bringing incense and money. Food and objects of meaning to the deceased are placed in the coffin. A priest then performs the burial ritual. Friends and family follow the coffin to the cemetery, taking with them a willow branch. This symbolizes the soul of the deceased and is carried back to the family altar where it becomes part of the ancestral spirits. Public prayers are said on the seventh, ninth and forty-ninth days after the burial and on the first and third anniversaries of the death.

On the surface, the practices and philosophies of Confucianism appear to differ greatly from those of its Indian counterparts. Confucianism is much more politically and socially oriented, as is Legalism.

Legalism

The Chinese often refer to themselves as Han or sons of Han. Taoist philosophy was in existence before one of the main defining periods in Chinese history, the Han Dynasty (206 BC–AD 220). At that time Confucianism was recognized as the state philosophy, there being an acceptance that the Chinese system of cultural values was considered to be of primary importance. Being Chinese is not based solely on race, however, but on systems of thought. Confucianism and Taoism have constantly vied for supremacy over the years, but there is a third system of belief – not a religion – which needs to be taken into account when tracing the path of Taoism. This is Legalism (*fa jia*).

Legalism is a purely political philosophy that neither has an interest in, nor focuses on, questions pertaining to the esoteric or the nature and purpose of existence. Ritual custom and ethics are totally ignored. In the belief that the only way to control human behaviour is through written law, it is concerned with the most successful and autocratic way of governing the people. Strong penalties are used as a deterrent against criminal activity, and obedience to the law is demanded.

The two principal sources of Legalist doctrine were the *Book of Lord Shang* and the *Han Fei-tzu*. Shang Yang, serving as governor of the state of Qin which unified China in 221 BC, teaches that the purpose of laws is to maintain the reliability of the state. People are innately selfish and ignorant and all rival philosophies are to be suppressed.

It was Han Fei-tzu (d. 233 BC) who drew together the various strands of Legalism. He had been taught by the Confucianist Hsun-tzu, who claimed that people were basically evil but could be guided towards goodness. Han Fei-tzu adopted and developed Hsun-tzu's misanthropic perspective and taught that people were so inherently bad that they could only be controlled by strong government and strict laws. His doctrine stated that these laws must enable the ruler to govern effectively and without leniency, that the ruler must conduct himself with great cunning, and remain inscrutable at all times. He held that any text books apart from law books were useless and therefore must be destroyed – this ultimately led to a huge loss of sacred texts. The persecution of learned scholars was rife throughout; many Confucian philosophers lost their lives and Taoists either did their best not to interfere or remained unobtrusive.

Some of Han Fei-tzu's writings show that he seems to have been influenced by Taoism, but as a philosophy Legalism leaves too much room for violence and autocracy while trying to achieve its aims. In addition the practice of the ideas leads to a lack of integrity.

It was the Taoists' ability to remain inconspicuous which was their saving grace. By following Tao and not interfering they were able to preserve their practices in an oral form, if not as written material.

Chapter Five

Christianity

The earliest documented contact between China and Christianity occurred during the Tang Dynasty (AD 618–907) when the Nestorian monk (and also bishop) Alopen arrived in Xi'an in AD 635. Nestorianism held that there were two separate persons – one human and one divine – in the incarnate Christ. This doctrine could be easily adapted to embrace Taoist, Confucian and Buddhist terms. Some scholars of Chinese religions feel that this adaptation, particularly the use of Buddhist concepts, led to a dilution of the Christian message, and to Nestorianism becoming confused with yet another offshoot of Buddhism.

From that time on up to the present day, Christianity has attempted to challenge existing Chinese religious thought. There are five major aspects to this:

1. The existence of Nestorian Christianity, beginning during the Tang dynasty and continuing to a minor degree into the Middle Ages.

2. Christian communities were set up by Franciscan missionaries during the Yuan dynasty (AD 1279–1368).

3. New communities were started by Jesuit and other Catholic missionaries from 1583 until 1800.

4. From 1803 to 1949, both Protestant and Catholic communities came into being.

5. Following the Cultural Revolution in 1949, and up to the present day, Protestant and Catholic communities of native-born Chinese have continued to develop.

There has always been some difficulty in converting Chinese people to Christianity. This is partly because Christianity was associated in the popular mind with Western imperialism, but also because the Chinese way of thinking does not necessarily lend itself to the emotional response inherent in Christianity. Some minor kings, as well as the mothers and wives of emperors, became Christians but no emperor ever converted to Christianity. While the concept of Father and Son is inherent in Christianity, it does not quite reflect the family values and loyalties in Chinese religions.

The cultural input of some 5,000 years and the belief systems and rituals thus generated lend themselves more readily to what has been popularly called folk religion, but which can perhaps be more correctly described as a way of life. Many of these religions were local, often based on native gods, and served small communities. They often incorporated elements of Buddhism, but owed more to Taoism, since the principles and rituals suited the Chinese way of thought.

Shintoism

One other Asian religion which deserves a mention, although it exists only in Japan, is Shintoism. It is similar to Taoism in that it concentrates on the power or spirit of natural phenomena as its main focus. The practice of Shinto consists chiefly of worshipping, appeasing and working with *kami* – this is a huge pantheon of gods or spirits which range from the local deities of mountains or streams to the sun goddess Amaterasu.

A *kami* might loosely be termed the 'spirit' or essence of any aspect of life which has its own identity and vital force (*tama*). Personifications of natural phenomena and particular places are designated as *kami*, important individuals could be sanctified and ancestors revered as such. Those who were believed to have special qualities, such as the emperor, have been regarded as living *kami*.

Two types of practice predominate:

- honouring the *kami* through prayer and offerings

- averting their wrath by cleansing oneself of impurity

Various stages of human life are also marked by Shinto ceremonies:

- a baby's first visit to its *kami* soon after its birth

- the *Shichi-go-san* (Seven-Five-Three) festival on November 15 each year when five-year-old boys and three- and seven-year-old girls visit shrines to pray for good health

- the traditional wedding ceremony

Shinto originated as a practical religion in an agricultural society based on seasonal cycles, and many of the ceremonies reflect this. Food offerings – such as rice, sake, fish, vegetables and fruit – as well as offerings of pine branches with white paper strips attached, frequently feature in the more important Shinto ceremonies.

Purity is important in the Shinto religion which regards death, disease, blood and dirt as obnoxious to the *kami*. Many rituals are performed to purge these aspects which are known as *kegare*. Blood was regarded as a particular contamination and women who were menstruating had to be kept away from the shrines – indeed women were once banned from many sacred mountains which were regarded as the god's body. The sick, wounded or recently bereaved were also traditionally barred from shrine precincts.

The earliest Shinto holy places were initially beautiful or striking places, often designated by a plaited straw rope or a wooden gate, the *torii*. It was only later that actual buildings were established. Shrines usually contain a sacred object (such as a sword, mirror or stone) which serves as the 'body' of the *kami*, similar to the symbolism seen in Chinese alchemy which we will explore later.

Many of the *kami* were supposedly born from the *misogi* (ablutions) of the ancestral deity Izanagi as he purified himself after visiting hell. Such cleansing is still seen in many modern-day healing techniques, including the regeneration of a more positive energy.

Buddhism, Confucianism and Taoism all migrated to Japan in the sixth century AD. As a result, the Shinto religion acquired an identity of its own with *kami* being accepted, in the case of Buddhism, as the reincarnation of Buddha. This process was aided in AD 743 when Amaterasu revealed herself as an aspect of the cosmic Buddha Vairocana. It was not until 1868 that Buddhism and the Shinto religion once again became separate entities by government decree.

As with so many religions which have their origins in folk practices, small family altars, roadside effigies and elaborate shrines are all suitable for worshipping the *kami*. The Shinto religion is organized parochially and residents of a particular area usually give allegiance to a local shrine. Each shrine has an annual festival (*Rei-sai*) which is marked by progressing noisily around the area with a *mikoshi* – a portable replica of the shrine. Even today, prayers are often said for any new venture. The Shinto religion is an integral part of social structure in Japan and the priesthood often passes from father to son. Their families may thus acquire status within their local community.

Both Shinto and Taoism show remarkable similarities in their beliefs which cannot always be explained by any possible merging of the two religions. It is more likely to arise from the acceptance of perceived principles of correct behaviour common to all races. The difference between them is that Shinto arose from the practical application of the beliefs whereas Taoism arose initially from a philosophy about the beliefs.

Although in essence more self-oriented, these same principles of correct behaviour are also seen in Hinduism and Buddhism. However the main belief behind all of the Eastern religions is their striving for order and balance. Confucianism strives for order and balance through *Jen* and *Li*, while Hinduism and Buddhism use Yogas and the Eightfold Path. The balance and order brought about by these different practices extends to a greater purpose – the achievement of a higher form of enlightenment.

The Taoist religion also demonstrates this search for balance, which is inherent in the understanding of *Yin* and *Yang*. 'Enlightenment' is of a slightly different form however, in that the Taoist wishes to achieve 'Immortality' or the 'lightening' of his being so that he becomes literally a 'being of light'. Such a concept is not perhaps seen to such an extent in the Graeco-Roman or Judeo-Christian religions, except in the Mystery religions, when purification takes place through various initiations.

What is shared by all these religions is the idea of a single unit giving rise to duality as laid down in the cosmology first put forward by the Greek philosopher Pythagoras:

The principle of all things is the monad or unit; arising from this monad the undefined dyad or two serves as material substratum to the monad, which is cause; from the monad and the undefined dyad spring numbers; from numbers, points; from points, lines; from lines, plane figures; from plane figures, solid figures; from solid figures, sensible bodies, the elements of which are four, fire, water, earth and air.

(Diogenes Laertius, Vitae Philosophorum VIII, 24)

THOUGHTS AND IDEAS

Just because I have enjoyed exploring the worlds religions,
I do not expect everybody to do the same. However,
the quotations I have chosen seem to fit in so well with
Taoist thought that I have included them for comparison.
Perhaps now is the time to widen your horizons a little bit.

Circling around each other like yin and yang themselves, Taoism and
Confucianism represent the two indigenous poles of the Chinese
character. Confucius represents the classical, Lao Tzu the romantic.
Confucius stresses social responsibility, Lao Tzu praises spontaneity
and naturalness. Confucius' focus is on the human, Lao Tzu's on
what transcends the human. As the Chinese themselves say,
Confucius roams within society, Lao Tzu wanders beyond. Something
in life reaches out in each of these directions, and Chinese civilization
would certainly have been poorer if either had not appeared.
Smith, Houston. *The World's Religions*

Therefore the phenomena of the three worlds (of desire, of form
and of non-form) are mind made. Without mind, then there is
practically no objective existence. Thus all existence arises from
imperfect notions in our mind all differences are differences of the
mind, but the mind cannot see itself, for it has no form. We should
know that all phenomena are created by the imperfect notions in the
finite mind; therefore all existence is like a reflection in the mirror,
without substance, only a phantom of the mind. When the finite
mind acts, then all kinds of things arise; when the finite mind ceases
to act then all kinds of things cease.
Tibetan Book of the Dead

Chapter Five

He who sees inaction in action and action in inaction,
he is wise among men; he is a Yogi and performer of
all actions.
The Bhagavad Gita

He whose undertakings are all devoid of desires and (selfish)
purposes, and whose actions have been burnt
by the fire of knowledge, – him the wise call a sage.
The Bhagavad Gita

Abandon nothing. Take up nothing. Rest, abide in yourself,
just as you are.
Abhinavagupta

O ye Knowledge-Holding Deities, pray hearken unto me;
Lead me on the path, out of your great love.
When (I am) wandering in the Sangrisara,
because of intensified propensities,
On the bright light-path of the Simultaneously-born Wisdom
May the bands of Heroes, the Knowledge-Holders, lead me;
May the bands of the Mothers, the Dakinis, be (my) rearguard;
May they save me from the fearful ambuscades of the Bardo,
And place me in the pure Paradise Realm.
Tibetan Book of the Dead

When the Tao was lost, its characteristics appeared. When its characteristics were lost, benevolence appeared. When benevolence was lost, righteousness appeared. When righteousness was lost, ceremonies appeared. Ceremonies are but the unsubstantial flowers of the Tao, and the commencement of disorder.

The Sufi does not consider life as different from business, but he sees how real business can be achieved in the best manner. The symbol of the mystics of China was a branch laden with fruit in their hand. What does it mean? It means that the purpose of life is to arrive at that stage where every moment becomes fruitful. And what does fruitful mean? Does it mean fruits for oneself? No, trees do not bear fruit for themselves, but for others. True profit is not that profit which one makes for oneself. True profit is that which one makes for others. After attaining all that one wants to attain, be it earthly or heavenly, what is the result of it all? The result is only this, that all that one has attained, that one has acquired, whether earthly or heavenly, one can place before others.

Chapter Five

The noble bodhisattva Avalokiteshvara practicing a deep practice of the perfection of wisdom perceived: five constituents. And he saw them as void of any existence on their own. Here, Sariputra, the form is emptiness, emptiness is just the form. Emptiness is not different from the form and the form is not different from emptiness. What is the form, that is emptiness; what is emptiness, that is the form. And just so it is with feeling, perception, mental impulses and consciousness. Here, Sariputra, all the phenomena have the emptiness as the characteristic. not arisen, not destroyed, not defiled, not purified, not lacking, not complete. Therefore, Sariputra, in emptiness, there is no form, no feeling, no perception, no mental impulses, no consciousness. No eye, ear, nose, tongue, body, mind. No form, sound, scent, taste, touchable, mind-object. No eye element..., until we come to: no consciousness-element. No ignorance, no extinction of ignorance..., until we come to: no old age and death, no extinction of old age and death. No suffering, arising, cessation, way. No knowledge, no attainment, no non-attainment. Therefore, Sariputra, it is because of bodhisattva's non-attainment that he dwells without the hindrances of the mind, having resorted to the perfection of wisdom. Because of non-existence of the hindrances of the mind, he is not frightened, he has crossed over distortions, at the end he will attain Nirvana. All the Buddhas existing in the three times, having resorted to the perfection of wisdom, have fully awakened to the highest and right awakenment. Therefore one should know: the perfection of wisdom as the great mantra, the mantra of great knowledge, the highest mantra, the unequalled mantra, pacification of all suffering. It is a truth – because it could not be wrong. The mantra was proclaimed in the Perfection of Wisdom. [It sounds] as follows: "Gate Gate Paragate Parasamga(Te) Bodhi Svaha."

The Sutra On The Heart Of The Perfection Of Wisdom

With Confucius and Mencius, Hsun Tzu was one of the outstanding
philosophical figures of the Chou dynasty era. His exact dates are
not known, but he flourished approximately 298–238 B.C.
Rites require us to treat both life and death with attentiveness. Life is
the beginning of man, death is his end. When a man is well off both
at the end and the beginning, the way of man is fulfilled.

Hence the gentleman respects the beginning and is carefully attentive
to the end. To pay equal attention to the end as well as to the
beginning is the way of the gentleman and the beauty of rites and
righteousness.

Y. P. Mei, in *Sources of Chinese Tradition*

All such parallels as these tend to strengthen our opinion that the
greater part of the symbolism nowadays regarded peculiarly
Christian or Jewish seems to be due to adaptations from Egyptian
and Eastern religions. They suggest too that the thought forms and
processes of Orient and of Occident are fundamentally, much alike-
that, despite differences of race and creed and of physical and social
environment, the nations of mankind are, and have been since time
immemorial, mentally and spiritually one.

Tibetan Book of the Dead

The Ling Pao school did not identify itself through specific symbols
or logos. However, there are interesting visual forms associated with
Ling Pao ritual. In another ritual the priest will sprinkle his sword with
water. The water represents water from heaven and the
sword is the demon-conquering sword of Chang Tao-ling,
the first heavenly master.

Chapter Six:

The Five Elements
of Tao

In many respects the teachings of both Lao Tse and Chuang Tse were not new. While they are put forward in a new and, for the time, innovative way they were actually based on principles which were already well known and loved throughout China.

Yin Yang and Five Elements

In the *I Ching*, which predates the scriptures attributed to Lao Tse, the two terms *yin* and *yang* take their meanings from the slopes of a mountain – shaded (north) and sunny (south) respectively. Through time, following this idea of shade and light, the two terms came to describe what might be called in Nature, as the Chinese understood it, a natural order: Heaven and Earth; the cold, passive aspect and a warm, active aspect; any two distinct polarities and finally, the feminine and the masculine. The idea that one divides into two – but at the same time remains whole – is a basic concept in all philosophical, scientific, and religious thought in China. However, in the West the concept was not well understood until C.G. Jung's work on archetypes and symbolism became common knowledge, although the idea of polarity had been appreciated by those whose lives were ruled by the cycle of the seasons and the daily round of light and dark.

**Diagram of Ultimatelessness which shows how
Yin Yang and the Five Elements inter-relate**

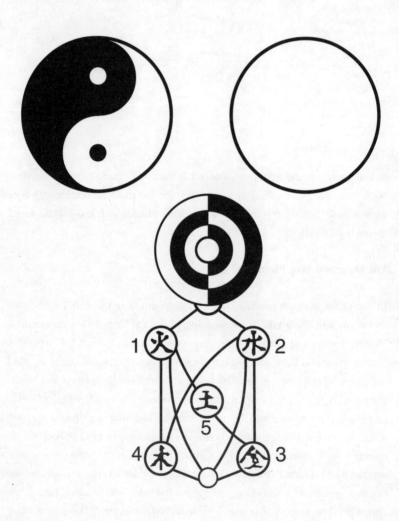

These principal cosmic forces or influences could, according to the Chinese, then further be classified according to the 'Five Elements,' or 'Five Phases' (*wu-hsing*) theory. This theory was put forward in the *Hung-fan* (Great Norm), a treatise inserted in the *Shu ching* (Classic of History). Each element was assigned a number, as can be also be seen in the list below. They were:

1. Water
2. Fire
3. Wood
4. Metal
5. Earth

Earth was defined as central and neutral; the four other elements were further classified as either *yin* or *yang* and corresponded to the four major directions and to the four seasons. Thus, spring and summer were both *yang* and corresponded, respectively, to wood and east, fire and south; autumn and winter were *yin* and corresponded to metal and west, water and north. In addition, the elements were symbolized by the five basic colours.

Element	Colour
Water	Black
Fire	Red
Wood	Green
Metal	White
Earth	Yellow

In fact, it is possible to list all manifestations of Nature – for instance, directions, flavours, foodstuffs, human activities, the organs of the body, seasons – under one or another of the Five Elements. We shall explore this more fully in the next chapter. It was – and indeed still is in modern day Chinese medicine – important to the individual that the elements remain in proper balance and relationship to one another.

Added to the symbolism of the Five Elements were four animals which often appeared in representations of sacred space and today are seen in the use of *Feng Shui*: the dragon to the east, the red bird or phoenix to the south, the white tiger to the west, and the tortoise, enlaced by a snake, to the north.

Symbols of I Ching

The *I Ching*, which is at least 5,000 years old, was originally a manual of explanation of the entire laws of the universe, and only later became a book of divination. It was probably studied by Confucius and was much loved by the Taoists, particularly because the symbolism uses so many natural forms. If we are to live in harmony with Nature then we must have some information as to how to do this in the most effective way possible and this was the basis of the *I Ching*. Unbroken lines represent *yang* and broken lines represent *yin*. When these lines are built up three at a time, we obtain eight trigrams which form a series of symbols, ideagrams or diagrams. These are given evocative names which represent forces in nature:

The Creative (Yang)

The Keeping Still (Mountain)

The Receptive (Yin)

The Gentle (Wind)

The Arousing (Thunder)

The Clinging (Fire)

The Abysmal (Water)

The Joyous (Lake)

The combination of any two trigrams gives us one of sixty-four possible hexagrams (six-line figures). It is said that within these sixty-four hexagrams lies the answer to every possible question that man can possibly have. Trigrams indicate the combination of separate principles into a coherent whole, while hexagrams suggest a more analytical approach. In other words, hexagrams allow us to analyse the whole question while the trigrams allow us to view the components. Individual lines give an explanation of the subtle energies at work.

Ch'ien and *k'un* – the first and second hexagrams of the *I Ching* (or Book of Changes) represent *yang* and *yin* – two polarities. The *ch'ien* hexagram consists of six *yang* (unbroken) lines composed of two *ch'ien* trigrams of the *yang* lines. This is therefore pure *yang*, Heaven and the creative principle. The *k'un* hexagram consists of six broken lines and thus two *k'un* trigrams of three *yin* lines. This symbolises pure *yin*, the Earth and receptive principle:

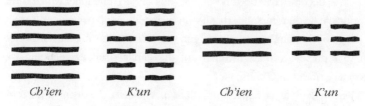

| *Ch'ien* | *K'un* | *Ch'ien* | *K'un* |

In the Taoist view, the world is an expression of the Tao – that is, the One in which *yin* and *yang* intermingle with the primordial *chi* (energy). Heaven and Earth actually manifested through the separation of *yin* and *yang*, and their continual merging and demerging caused the Ten Thousand things – that is, all things and creatures – (*wan-wu*) to appear.

A translation of a Taoist text – *The Experience of the Golden Flower* – contains the following passage:

> Before Heaven and Earth were separate, there was only the indefinable one. The one was divided and yin and yang came into existence. That which received yang-ch'i rose up bright and clear and became heaven; that which received yin-ch'i sank down heavy and obscure and became Earth; and that which received both yin-ch'i and yang-ch'i in right proportions became man.

Ch'ien and *k'un*, being pure energy, are considered to be transformational and are thought of as being the 'parents' of the remaining hexagrams, which are combinations of *yin* and *yang* lines. *K'un* represents the Great Mother at her most receptive and *Ch'ien* The Father, sovereign or Ruler at his most penetrative. In the *Tao Te Ching* the Tao is given the honour of being the feminine principle, the mother of the world. Tao gives birth to all physical manifestations, and its *te*, or nourishing virtue, preserves them and allows them to grow into wisdom. At one point in the *Tao Te Ching* the Tao is called the 'spirit of the valley' and the 'mysterious female'. The Tao is beyond the grasp of the senses and is imperceptible – it is 'no-thingness'. But from 'nothingness' (*wu*) comes the visible world (*yu*) and from this the tangible world is born.

This suggests that at one and the same time everything arises from *yin* and *yang* – one becomes two becomes many. (It is easy to remember which is the *yin* principle if you remember that both *yin* and feminine contain 'in'.) Since the image of the family is very strong in the *I Ching*, the trigrams are often seen to represent various members of the family structure, echoing the importance of this in Chinese life.

When we look at Taoist alchemy (*nei-tan*, *wei-tan*) *ch'ien* and *k'un* refer respectively to the furnace and cauldron (melting pot) and, on a personalized level, the head and stomach of the practitioner. *Ch'ien* is also associated with the external features of the physical body such as the ears, eyes, nose, mouth and tongue, whilst *k'un* is said to be related to the internal organs such as the heart, lungs, kidneys and pancreas – that 'contained' within the body. The 'superior man' mentioned so often in the *I Ching* is the one who has achieved as perfect a balance as possible between *yin* and *yang*, his inner and outer self, thought and emotion.

Chih-jen – 'perfected human being' – is one of the names used by Chuang Tse to describe his ultimate human being. A perfected human being has balanced his polarities and become conscious of unity with the Tao. He has thus freed himself from earthly limitations and concepts. This is similar to the principle of non-attachment as seen in Buddhism. One translation of the

Chuang Tse texts describes the Perfect Man in this way:

> The Perfect Man is a spiritual being. Were the ocean itself scorched up, he would not feel hot. Were the Milky Way frozen hard, he would not feel cold. Were the mountains to be riven with thunder and the great deep to be thrown up by storm, he would not tremble. In such case, he would mount upon the clouds of heaven and, driving the sun and moon before him, would pass beyond the limits of this external world where death and life have no victory over man – how much less what is bad for him.

Man is certainly subject to changes and transformations but essentially he is a reflection of the universe, a microcosm, and should therefore be capable of remaining unmoved and balanced. His head is round like Heaven, his organs correspond to, or are ruled by, different parts of the universe and his feet are square like the earth. This system of classification based on the Five Elements theory makes it possible to describe the microcosm and its conformity or dissonance by means of the rhythms of the natural world.

When all is calm and at rest the elements of positive and/or negative – *yin* and *yang* – build up. When there is movement these elements will eventually break down and the energy will be transformed. When a climax is reached or everything is unbalanced, the energy transforms into its opposite and the whole cycle begins again. Thus, growth is followed by decay which is again followed by growth and so on. It is this acceptance of the inevitability of these changes within what in the *I Ching* is called the World of Senses – the tangible world – that leads us to explore the World of Thought, which is the domain of ideas, motives and wishes; those things beyond the five senses. With a deeper understanding of the World of Thought we can walk our own Tao more successfully.

Just as the moon waxes and wanes so there are times when there is more energy available to allow things to happen in the correct way, times when we should remain still, as well as times when we must realise that nothing needs to be done. While it is possible to consult the *I Ching* as to the right course of action, it is also possible to consult it as to the correct timing of our actions. Thus we will be acting within the natural flow of things and be in accord with the Tao.

In understanding this requirement to be within the flow, it is imperative to the Taoist that he takes good care of his own energies. We can see that he must nourish his own 'life spark' to the best of his ability. To maximise the potency of his energies he must be sustained by the five flavours and should eat according to the seasons of the year. His internal hygiene needs to be of the highest order and his health should be maintained to the best of his ability. To do this he is required to practise a set of physical exercises designed to maximise the energy that he has been given and if something does go wrong he is honour bound to put it right by the best means at his disposal. He must also give himself the best possible environment in which to operate.

In simpler times when everything seemed more miraculous, the boundaries between medicine and magic became blurred, as did those between philosophy and religion, and it is the use of various related techniques that we shall explore within the next chapters. One of the ways in which the Taoist can understand his environment and receive guidance as to how he should conduct his life is by consulting the *I Ching*.

Consulting the I Ching

When consulting the *I Ching* to determine a course of action, the construction of the hexagram allows the person asking the question to concentrate fully on the matter in hand and make a strong link with the energies and forces which lie behind the situation. Initially, using materials which were readily available to the Chinese, the hexagram was constructed through a complicated process of throwing and counting yarrow stalks. Later this evolved into using three coins. (These three coins appear again as good luck charms and wealth bringers in the art of *Feng Shui*.)

The obverse (head) of each coin is given a value of three (odd numbers are considered to be *yang*), while the reverse (tail) is worth two (even numbers are *yin*). Three coins, shaken in the hand like dice and thrown onto a flat surface, will therefore add up to a total of either six, seven, eight or nine (a mixture of heads and tails). The coins are thrown six times in all, giving a hexagram of six lines. Hexagrams are always inscribed from the bottom of the page to the top, in accordance with written Chinese language.

The numbers seven and eight represent 'young' – that is energetic – *yang* and *yin*, respectively. Seven and eight add a plain *yang* ▬ or a plain *yin* ▬▬ line to the hexagram. The numbers six and nine, in turn, represent 'mature' yin and yang, and are called 'changing lines'. The appearance of these changing lines suggests that there must be some kind of alteration in circumstances before a balance can be established.

Since, according to the Tao, everything eventually becomes its opposite these weak lines – as they are sometimes known – are in the process of alteration. If any changing lines are involved in our original hexagram we eventually finish up with two hexagrams; the first hexagram shows the present state of affairs while the second hexagram, after the changes have been made, shows what will be the future state of affairs. This illustrates an important aspect of the theory of *yin* and *yang* – that of return – and allows the *I Ching* to be used as a tool for divination.

Hexagrams

On the following pages are some typical hexagrams numbered according to the *I Ching* which might be cast to answer specific questions. The first stands without any need for 'changing lines' and it is enough to have only a judgement. The judgement in this case is enough information. The second and third hexagrams give the interpretation of the lines were any of them to show the need for action.

The question asked might have been along the lines of 'How can I best maximise my opportunities?'

8. Pi/Holding Together (Union)

above *K'an* The Abysmal, Water

below *K'un* The Receptive, Earth

The Judgement
Holding Together brings good fortune.
Inquire of the oracle once again
Whether you possess sublimity, constancy, and perseverance;
Then there is no blame.
Those who are uncertain gradually join.
Whoever comes too late
Meets with misfortune.

This is a hexagram which often is thrown when reappraisal is necessary. The various changing lines give the course of action to be taken. The symbolism is easy to understand if one remembers the structure of Chinese society which was very hierarchical.

24. Fu/Return (The Turning Point)

above *K'un* The Receptive, Earth

below *Chên* The Arousing, Thunder

The Judgement
Return. Success.
Going out and coming in without error.
Friends come without blame.
To and Fro goes the way.
On the seventh day comes return.
It furthers one to have somewhere to go.

The Image
Thunder within the earth:
The image of The Turning Point.
Thus the kings of antiquity closed the passes
At the time of solstice.
Merchants and strangers did not go about,
And the ruler
Did not travel through the provinces.

The Lines
Change at the beginning means:
Return from a short distance.
No need for remorse.
Great good fortune.

Change in the second place means:
Quiet return. Good fortune.

Change in the third place means:
Repeated return. Danger. No blame.

Change in the fourth place means:
Walking in the midst of others,
One returns alone.

Change in the fifth place means:
Noble-hearted return.
No remorse.

Change at the top means:
Missing the return. Misfortune.
Misfortune from within and without.
If armies are set marching in this way,
One will in the end suffer a great defeat,
Disastrous for the ruler of the country.
For ten years
It will not be possible to attack again.

The following hexagram might have been thrown in response to a supplementary question.

55. Fêng/Abundance (Fullness)

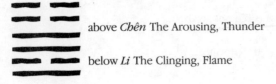

above *Chên* The Arousing, Thunder

below *Li* The Clinging, Flame

The Judgement
Abundance has success.
The king attains abundance.
Be not sad.
Be like the sun at midday.

The Image
Both thunder and lightning come:
The image of Abundance.
Thus the superior man decides lawsuits
And carries out punishments.

The Lines
Change at the beginning means:
When a man meets his destined ruler,
They can be together ten days,
And it is not a mistake.
Going meets with recognition.

Change in the second place means:
The curtain is of such fullness
That the polestars can be seen at noon.
Through going one meets with mistrust and hate.
If one rouses him through truth,
Good fortune comes.

Change in the third place means:
The underbrush is of such abundance
That the small stars can be seen at noon.
He breaks his right arm. No blame.

Change in the fourth place means:
The curtain is of such fullness
That the polestars can be seen at noon.
He meets his ruler, who is of like kind.
Good fortune.

Change in the fifth place means:
Lines are coming,
Blessing and fame draw near.
Good fortune.

Change at the top means:
His house is in a state of abundance.
He screens off his family.
He peers through the gate
And no longer perceives anyone.
For three years he sees nothing.
Misfortune.

T'ai Chi

Out of the Tao emerges The One, out of The One comes Two, Two gives birth to Three, everything else comes from Three.

This is the *T'ai Chi* symbol, which represents the balance of *yin* and *yang* in the universe. It presents in pictorial form a reminder of many of the basic principles of Taoist philosophy. For the purist this is really the only way that it can be drawn so that it performs this function.

The main thing to remember is that yin is the dark, cold, female, introvert, passive side of life and in the *T'ai Chi* symbol it is shown as the black area. Yang is the light, warm, male, extrovert, active aspect and it is shown as the white area. There are two particularly important points to remember. Firstly, the *T'ai Chi* symbol suggests that everything in the Universe (the 'Ten Thousand Things' of the *Tao Te Ching*) contains two aspects – a basic duality. These aspects do not conflict with one another but fit together to make one complete whole. Within each polarity, however, lies the seed of its opposite (the two small dots) and in due course, as the cycles of life progress, the polarities turn into one another. This, of course, is Change.

Secondly, Taoist philosophy is based on the idea that everything moves in natural cycles. These cycles of life – days, months, years and even hours – can all be represented by the circle of the *T'ai Chi*. The flow of all time and energy is indicated by the way the *yin* and the *yang* areas increase and decrease as they progress around the symbol.

Highest Yang

Increasing Yang

Increasing Yin

Highest Yin

The four seasons – Spring, Summer, Autumn and Winter – are not only part of the cycles but, according to the available warmth and energy, are also linked to *yin* and *yang* as well as to the directions of the compass.

Spring	the time of new growth	increasing *Yang*	**East**
Summer	the time of greatest heat	highest *Yang*	**South**
Autumn	as the year cools	increasing *Yin*	**West**
Winter	the coldest time	highest *Yin*	**North**

In the *T'ai Chi* symbol, the seasons are assigned to the appropriate areas of *yin* and *yang*:

Summer

Spring *Autumn*

Winter

The Chinese Compass Directions

The Chinese compass is based on the same four main directions as in the Western world, except that in Chinese thought the South is considered to be the main direction, since warmth comes from the South. Shown at the top of Chinese compasses, it is therefore at the top of the *T'ai Chi* symbol.

As mentioned above, the *T'ai Chi* symbol is linked to the compass directions, through the seasons:

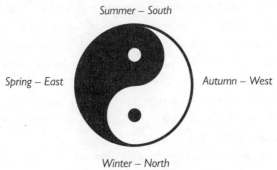

Summer – South

Spring – East *Autumn – West*

Winter – North

This natural flow of energy is inherent in all the systems of healing, exercise and self-management which have their roots in Tao, but probably none more so than in the art of *Feng Shui*.

Feng Shui

> *All things arise from the Tao – they are formed out of Matter, they are shaped by their environment.*

One of the most important adjustments which can be made, as we find our own Tao, is to the environment in which we live and to our own personal space. As we reach an internal peace we create tranquillity around us, but equally our environment must nurture us. For the Taoist practitioner this means understanding both our living space and our own subtle aura – or energy field – created by our own vitality.

Scientific discoveries which have been made during the twentieth century mean that we are becoming more and more aware of the constantly shifting fields of energy through which we move in our daily lives. Today we call them electromagnetic fields and talk of 'adjusting the flow'. This concept of energy fields is by no means new, however, because the fact that there was subtle movement between the two polarities of *yin* and *yang* (negative and positive) was recognized as far back as 5,000 years ago in the *I Ching* (The Book of Changes).

The art of *Feng Shui* (literally meaning wind and water) gives an understanding of these energies and movements, both tangible and intangible; it is the art of correct placement. Good *Feng Shui* practitioners will understand the processes of transformation, both internal and external, which can take place when one is in tune with one's environment and will do their best to balance the external energies in a way that is appropriate for the task in hand, whether that is creating a harmonious home, a productive working space or a healing vibration.

To understand the theory of *Feng Shui* we must first redefine our understanding of divination. Divination – in this case using the *I Ching* and the hexagrams as a tool – means being able to ascertain the most likely course of events should we be able to adjust any or all of the energies, when we are out of balance. It consists of working with the flow of essential energy and making very subtle adjustments when necessary, so that we approach the ideal or the divine as closely as possible.

Feng Shui can have an effect on every aspect of our lives. The way it is applied can be either beneficial or detrimental (or both) to the way we live and to the surrounding environment. It is by no means a game or fad, but it is a way to live in harmony with Nature, as it is understood in the Tao, so that the energy surrounding us works for us rather than against us.

In the West, *Feng Shui* has not yet achieved the status of a science, since its principles cannot yet be proved by scientific method – although it does require mathematical calculation. Neither a religion, a philosophy nor a belief system, it puts into practice tools and techniques which enable us to reach the Tao and remain within it. A system which has stood the test of time naturally changes to keep pace with knowledge and it is perhaps unfortunate that the superstitious 'silly' side of the wealth of information available to practitioners of *Feng Shui* has received so much publicity in recent times. The judicious placing and use of mirrors, wind-chimes of a certain type of material or crystals hung in windows do enhance the available energy, but only when carried out according to strict laws of correspondence.

Over the centuries many different schools of *Feng Shui* have developed. The basic principles are broadly the same, though each school has a slightly different focus. There are three main schools in existence today:

Form School

This school focuses on the features of the surrounding landscape and the correct use of the positioning of buildings – and, in former times, burial sites – to gain protection from inauspicious winds (*feng*) and provide adequate water to sustain life (*shui*) though the latter's energy can be unpredictable.

Chapter Six

A site or building, by tradition, needs the protective or energizing force of particular animals. We have already seen the four animals that guard the directions; the dragon to the east, the red bird or phoenix to the south, the tiger to the west and the tortoise, enlaced by a snake, to the north. If landforms such as the contours of the hills or other natural features surrounding the site can be seen as such symbols, then the location is extremely fortunate. The building is protected and/or energized according to its position. The art of the practitioner is to minimize or deflect bad energy (*sha*) and bring beneficial energy (*chi*) to the establishment.

Compass School

This style of *Feng Shui* uses the eight major trigrams of the *I Ching* and relates them to the eight principal points of the Compass. These are laid out to form the eight-sided figure called the *Pa Kua* which is used to interpret the favourable and unfavourable locations, not just for buildings as a whole but also house floor plans and room layouts. The *Feng Shui* practitioner will advise on the correct placement of objects within each 'mansion' and will often advise also on colour. The Compass school may also use the Flying Star system which takes into account the astrological significances (calculated according to the Chinese system) of the time at which the house was built.

As we have already seen in the discussion of the *Tai Chi* (the Yin Yang symbol) the Chinese compass works with the South at the top of the diagram. Just as with Western astrology and magical systems, in Chinese thought each direction is focused on certain important areas of life or significances. Each compass point and trigram has its own 'Mansion' within which are held the energies of that direction, to be drawn on or mitigated at will by the able practitioner.

Opposite in table form, are the significances of each of the eight trigrams. These are, in order, Family position, Element, Polarity, Colour, Season, Area of Life (most important) and, finally, the Shape which enhances the energy of that section.

The Five Elements of Tao

The Pa Kua (or Ba Gua)
The Eight Mansions Theory

SE

Trigram: Sun (1st daughter)
Wood
(Yin)
Light Green
Late Spring
Wealth, Prosperity
Rectangular

South

Trigram - Li (2nd daughter)
Fire
(Yang)
Red
Summer
Recognition, Fame, Popularity
Triangle

SW

Trigram - Kun (Mother)
Earth
(Yang)
Yellow
Late summer
Matriarch, Matrimony, Nurturing
Square

Trigram - Chen (1st son)
Wood
(Yang)
E Green
Spring
Family Health and Relationship
Rectangular

TAI CHI
Earth

Trigram - Tui (3rd daughter)
Metal
(Yin)
Gold, White **W**
Autumn
Descendants, Hobbies, Pleasures
Round

Trigram - Ken (3rd son)
Earth
(Yin)
Beige
Late Winter
Education, Knowledge
Square
NE

Trigram – Kan (2nd son)
Water
(Yin)
Black, Blue
Winter
Career
Wavy
North

Trigram - Ch'ien (Head of family)
Metal
(Yang)
Grey, Silver
Late Autumn
Patrons, Mentor, Helpful people
Round
NW

129

Black Hat Sect School

This is a more modern version of *Feng Shui* which has its roots not only in traditional *Feng Shui* but also in Tibetan Buddhism and Taoism. In this school, the *Pa Kua* (often called the *Ba Gua*) is used, but it is based on the direction of the front door of the building, rather than the compass directions. The house or room is divided into eight sectors, similar to the Eight Mansions, each one having a bearing on an aspect of life that might need enhancing.

In the words of the sage:

> It is only the individual possessed of supreme sincerity who can give full development to his nature. Able to give full development to his nature, he can give full development to the nature of all men. Able to give full development to the nature of all men, he can give full development to the nature of all things. Able to give full development to the nature of all things, he can assist the transforming and nurturing processes of Heaven and earth. Able to assist the transforming and nurturing processes of Heaven and earth, he may, with Heaven and earth, form a triad.

Opposite is a *Pa Kua* calculated for a house which has recently been purchased. Using Chinese astrological calculations, a 'fit' must be found between the occupants' life energy and the energy of the house. The energy of this house is very much in accord with the birth-date of one of the occupants, yet there are certain problems associated with it in that, for instance, the kitchen is in the 'Death' area. This means that either the kitchen must be moved, which is not immediately practical, or certain changes must be made within the area to minimize risk. There are four helpful areas (Longevity, Prosperity, Health and Excellent) and four unhelpful areas (Death, Disaster, Irritation and Spooks – also known as the 'Six Curses'). There is a toilet in the house within the 'Spooks' area, but with a little thought this can be used to keep the area clear – one simply remembers to, quite literally, 'flush away' the negativity. Thus it can be seen that such an action follows the tenets of the Tao since one is living in harmony with what is available to be used. The diagram below has been drawn in accordance with the Western way of having south at the bottom of the diagram.

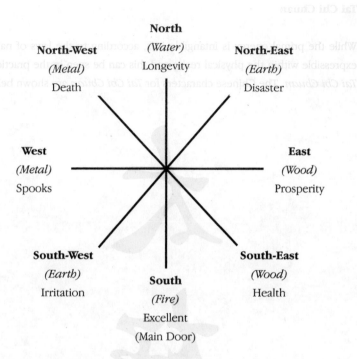

North
(Water)
Longevity

North-West
(Metal)
Death

North-East
(Earth)
Disaster

West
(Metal)
Spooks

East
(Wood)
Prosperity

South-West
(Earth)
Irritation

South
(Fire)
Excellent
(Main Door)

South-East
(Wood)
Health

Presenting *Feng Shui* in such a simplistic fashion in no way honours the art as it should be. It is much too complex a subject for that, and true practitioners will study for many years to perfect their skill and reach the state of Perfect Man. *Feng Shui* is one of the ways of the Tao which assists us to remain in harmony with ourselves and the environment. In order to appreciate the full force of being within the Tao we can seek to adopt the disciplines that will enable us to experience *wu chi* (primal energy) – an awesome power that pervades everything and is the One. Truly then:

It is beyond form, It is beyond sound, It is intangible.

Tai Chi Chuan

While the primal energy is intangible it is, according to the laws of nature, expressible within the physical realm and this can be seen in the practice of *Tai Chi Chuan*. The Chinese characters for *Tai Chi Chuan* are shown below.

The first character is 'tai', the literal meaning of which is extreme, great or supreme. The second character is 'chi', which means Ultimate or Polarity. So the literal translation is 'The Supreme Ultimate' or 'Extreme Polarity' – as in the two ends of a spectrum. We will look at the third character a little later.

We have already seen the *Tai Chi* expressed as the *yin yang* symbol, where it demonstrated the blending of negative and positive energy and their essential balance and interaction. As a philosophical term its origins actually stretch back some four thousand years, long before the *Tao Te Ching* was in existence. Dr. Nie Zhi-fei, a present-day philosopher, says:

> Tai-chi can be treated as the driving force of the universe, which generates two poles (Yang, Yin), then evolving the four phases (sky, earth, men, and matter), which then produce the eight sections (sky, earth, men, matter, time, space, material and spirit). They give rise to all kinds of activities in the earth.

It is important to note that *Chi*, meaning 'the Ultimate', is not quite the same as *chi*, meaning 'breath' or 'energy'. For ease of interpretation, however, we might consider the latter as a microcosm or reflection of the former. Both have the qualities of perpetual gentle movement, so the practice of *Tai Chi Chuan* is a mirroring of the subtle movement of the universe. The symbol is a static representation, while the practice lives and flows and is a dynamic presentation of essential energy.

Tradition has it that the *Tai Chi Chuan* eight basic postures are symbolised by the eight trigrams – *Chien, Kun, Kan, Li, Sun, Chen, Tui* and *Ken* respectively and their balance of *yin* and *yang*. These postures – Ward-Off (*Peng*), Roll-Back (*Lu*), Press (*Chi*), Push (*An*), Pull Down (*Tsai*) Split (*Lieh*), Elbow (*Chou*) and Shoulder-Strike (*Kao*) are slow motion movements. They follow the circular pattern of the *yin yang* (*Tai Chi*) symbol using open and closed postures, fullness and emptiness, and control (*Chuan* – the final character above) of mind and body working as one. Thus the practitioner is attempting to gain control of the very subtle forces which we have already encountered in the *yin yang* symbol.

Built on the basic eight postures are other intermediate ones. The whole form of 108 postures takes approximately twenty-five minutes to carry out in a completely relaxed yet focused way, and although many would nowadays see it as a purely therapeutic set of exercises – at times it even becomes the butt of unkind jokes – we do have to remember that the discipline was initially a training for the martial arts. The premise was that the practitioner first had to master himself, getting to know and understand the internal flow of energy. *Tai Chi Chuan* is the process which leads to internal energy – or *chi* – building up and, ultimately, leading to the development of the spirit.

Chang San-Feng, a Taoist hermit who is generally credited with founding the school of *Tai Chi* is reputed to have lived either during the Sung (AD 960–1279) or the Yuan dynasty (AD 1271–1368). According to popular belief, at one point he witnessed a snake engaged in combat with a particular bird, the crane. He was so impressed with the skilful way in which the snake was able to dodge and counter-attack the larger, apparently more powerful crane that he dreamed of the art of *Tai Chi* that night. The symbolism of this is interesting, since in Chinese lore the crane is seen as an intermediary between heaven and earth while the snake, in common with the dragon, is often taken as the highest spiritual power.

Certainly, *Tai Chi Chuan*, with its roots in Taoist philosophy, is a spiritual discipline as much as a physical one. The discipline was held in very high esteem by the royal court at various times, as a way of increasing the natural power of the body. Combining fighting stances with other more fluid dance or bird-like movements means that *Tai Chi* is a physical, artistically beautiful manifestation of Taoist principles.

In many ways *Tai Chi Chuan* (nowadays often shortened to *Tai Chi*) did not have to have a philosophy, because it demonstrated such inherent perfection. However, perhaps because it was so perfect there exists a huge body of writing and scholarly study which picks up on the Taoist philosophical thought behind the practice. The *Tao Te Ching* expresses the balance of energy in ways that speak directly to the *Tai Chi* practitioner, and *Tai Chi* expresses in movement what words cannot convey. Always there is the sense of contrast or of opposition, of yielding wherever feasible, of appreciating that force cannot prevail where there is nothing for it to meet. It is an example of *wu wei* (no-thingness or emptiness) in the true meaning of the word.

These following verses illustrate the central principle of *Tai Chi Chuan*, that of yielding to the opponent's force:

> Therefore the ancients say, 'Yield and overcome'.
> Is that an empty saying?

> The softest thing in the universe
> Overcomes the hardest thing in the universe.

> The hard and strong will fall
> The soft and weak will overcome them.

> The weak can overcome the strong;
> The supple can overcome the stiff.
> Under heaven everyone knows this,
> Yet no one puts it into practice.

Another verse demonstrates the principles of complementary forces:

> The heavy is the root of the light;
> The still is the master of unrest.
> To be light is to lose one's root.
> To be restless is to lose one's control.

> That which shrinks, Must first expand.
> That which fails, Must first be strong.
> That which is cast down, Must first be raised.

Just as it is impossible to grasp the Tao intellectually or through some logical procedure, the principles of *Tai Chi Chuan* can only ultimately be experienced intuitively. There is a kind of 'a-ha' experience when the body responds to the eternal flow, and a sense of rightness and poise when one remains in that flow. However much one practises, without that inner knowing there is no awareness of the symbolic meaning of the movements. This shift in consciousness allows most of the blocks to the awareness of more esoteric matters to be removed. As a result, we become reconnected to an original insight, the Tao, which allows us to gain access to, and is the working and the wonder of, the cosmos. Aldous Huxley describes this perfectly in his novel *Island*:

> No leaps, no high kicks, no running. The feet always firmly on the ground . . . movements intrinsically beautiful and at the same time charged with symbolic meaning. Thought taking shape in ritual and stylised gesture. The whole body transformed into a hieroglyph, a succession of hieroglyphs, of attitudes modulating from significance to significance, like a poem or a piece of music. Movements of the muscles representing movements of the consciousness . . . It's meditation in action; the metaphysics of the Mahayana expressed not in words, but through symbolic movements and gestures.

Chi Gung

Movement and exercise have always existed in the Chinese culture, even before the development of Taoism. *Chi Gung* is an exercise system that is some three thousand years old and we need to understand why it has stood the test of time. In earlier times philosophers were people who practised the art of meditation, and, in their efforts to live in accordance with natural principles, also practised exercise and medicine. *Chi Gung* was developed to satisfy this discipline. This holistic approach to their own well-being meant that they took responsibility for their own continuing good health and longevity. *Chi Gung* is a personal discipline that combines stillness, or gentle movement, with focused, regular breathing. We have seen *chi* defined elsewhere as breath – put simply this art means 'guiding the breath'. It is slightly more complex than that because it is actually the energy of the breath that is directed to either increase, balance, or control the *chi* (the essential life-force).

The understanding of the ordinary lay person is that breath goes into the lungs, oxygen is transferred to the bloodstream and waste products are expelled on exhalation. The *Chi Gung* practitioner, however, sees the process as much more subtle than that. Energy is transferred to the meridians (lines of power) within the body, bringing about a state of balance which leads naturally to a strengthening in the overall state of health and an increased resistance to illness.

Although there are many different styles of *Chi Gung*, the basic movements themselves are not terribly complex and are usually easy to learn. A *Chi Gung* Master will often, however, only teach his own more arcane knowledge to specifically chosen individuals – those whom he perceives will truly understand this very prized art.

Chi Gung can be divided into two main types: stationary exercises and moving exercises. Stationary exercises are practised either standing, sitting or lying down: the head and limbs of the body are held motionless. Moving exercises entail movement of the limbs and body. In addition, *Chi Gung* can be further classified as 'Soft' or 'Hard'. The former is used to maintain health and the latter is used in training for the martial arts. Advanced *Chi Gung* develops the *chi*, so that it is capable of leaving the body and can be used to ameliorate other people's illnesses – a kind of spiritual healing. However, it must be stressed that healing should not be attempted without the teaching of a competent master.

The *Chi Gung* art of deep breathing, recognizing the points of power on the meridians (as in acupuncture) and practising the simplest stances need initially take up no more than ten minutes per day. The benefits can be felt within a relatively short time. More prolonged practice obviously leads to greater competence and the more advanced exercises do require a fair amount of training.

Chi Gung is also a much-respected system of prevention, treatment and support for conditions such as those listed below.

Arthritis

Breast cancer

Diabetes

Eyesight Problems

Fatigue and Nerve Pain

Gastritis

Gynaecological Problems

Heart Disease

Infertility

Insomnia

Kidney Problems

Partial Paralysis

Physical Ageing

Rheumatism

Stress

Shown below are two easy exercises that demonstrate the simplicity of *Chi Gung*. The first is a variation on the natural standing position we saw originally in *Tai Chi Chuan* (thus demonstrating the common heritage of the two systems) which, when done properly, is comfortable for considerable lengths of time. The second exercise uses this stance for learning how to exercise control and direct power.

Horse or Horse Riding Stance

1. Stand comfortably for a few moments and, in your mind's eye, find your *tan tien* (a point of power in your abdomen about two inches below the solar plexus and three inches beneath the surface). It is from here that you can eventually learn to control your own energies.

2. When ready, place your feet together, then keeping the toes stationary, turn both heels outward as far as possible.

3. Keeping your heels stationary, lean slightly forward and straighten your feet.

4. Keeping the toes stationary, again turn both heels outward as far as possible.

5. Finally, with the heels remaining stationary, turn the toes to point forward and feet parallel to each other.

6. Ensure that your body weight is equally supported by each leg and sense that the soles of your feet are in firm contact with the ground. This sequence ensures that you are poised and at the same time properly connected with the earth's energies.

7. Hold the chest slightly in, as though making it concave but do not allow your spine to curve.

8. Keep your upper and lower back (full length of the spine) straight, relaxed but slightly extended.

9. Keep both hips level and maintain them in a natural position.

10. Do not push your buttocks out, slightly clench them instead.

11. There should be no tension in your shoulders (keep them relaxed and level) or in your elbows and wrists.

12. Loosen your upper arms with the armpits held slightly 'open'.

13. Rest both hands by your side in a natural position, with the fingers slightly tensed and separate from each other.

14. Keep your neck muscles relaxed but your head upright, neither leaning forwards or backwards, or slanting left or right.

15. Relax your jaws and keep your mouth partially closed with your lips gently touching one another. Touch the hard palate behind your upper teeth with the tip of your tongue. Breathe in and out gently through the nose.

16. Allow the eyelids to droop and look naturally downwards and forwards.

Tip: It is worthwhile practising each section of this exercise separately first to get a sense of how each part feels, before putting it all together as a coherent whole. The adoption of the stance soon becomes second nature.

Chapter Six

Draw a Bow to Shoot an Arrow

1. Assume the Horse Riding Stance.

2. While imagining that you are clasping a huge beachball to your chest, raise your hands to chest height with the palms facing inwards towards the body and the tips of the third fingers barely touching. This 'embraces the world' and opens the heart area.

3. Cross both arms in front of the chest with the right arm on the outside of the left arm.

4. Keep focused on the left hand throughout this part of the exercise. Curl the middle, ring and little finger of the left hand as though holding a bow string, but keep the forefinger extended forwards and the thumb pointed upwards.

5. Inhale as you open your left arm, raise it to shoulder height and extend it horizontally to the left. Push and stretch away your hand, palm and index finger. Imagine that your left palm is pressing flat against the wood of an archer's bow.

6. At the same moment, clench the right hand into a loose fist and pull it to the right of the body at shoulder height, in a horizontal movement.

7. Exhale as you release both fists and return the arms to a crossed position in front of the chest (this time, left arm on the outside of the right arm).

8. Repeat the exercise to the right side of the body.

This exercise helps with co-ordination and speed of reaction. As a means of directing energy at a desired goal it enables one to focus intention. If you remember that most schools of martial arts employ *Chi Gung* to increase the striking power of their fighting techniques, this exercise falls into place. Masters can perform extraordinary feats of strength and endurance by developing the use of *chi*. Self mastery is a prerequisite of working with Tao, and *Chi Gung* – often considered to be the mother of *Tai Chi* – works simultaneously at both a physical and spiritual level. The whole sequence of Eight Brocade exercises – from which the above two are taken – originated from the time of the Song dynasty (around the twelfth century AD). They are thought to have been developed by an army officer in order to maintain the internal strength and discipline of his troops.

Physically *Chi Gung* strengthens, relaxes and revitalizes the body. By opening and clearing the channels of *chi* the accumulated stress and negativity in the body is cleared away. As a result practitioners feel lighter, rejuvenated and more comfortable which in turn makes it easier to accept the benefits from a spiritual perspective. The practice will help you to focus and develop your awareness and insight into the deeper and more spiritual nature of yourself and Nature. This connection may be experienced as a meditative, expansive, deeply nurturing and relaxing state which leads on naturally to the exploration of the concept of *wu wei* or Emptiness, but before that happens we must have a fuller concept of how the Five Elements or Phases can give a sense of integration within a spiritual dimension.

THOUGHTS AND IDEAS

By now you will know that Tao can creep up on one unexpectedly.
Here it would in many ways be easier not to have words at all.
This is a 'doing' chapter when pictures or ideograms would
probably be more effective in communicating the richness of our
subject. Still, here are some words, so that you may form
your own pictures.

When enough earth is accumulated to make a mountain, wind
and rain arise. When much goodness is accumulated, spiritual
enlightenment comes of itself, and the sagely heart is attained.

Can you become a little child?
The child will cry all the day, without its throat becoming hoarse,
so perfect is the harmony of its physical constitution. It will keep
its fingers closed all day without relaxing their grasp. It will keep its
eyes fixed all day without their moving – so is it unaffected by
what is external to it. It walks it knows not whither; it rests
where it is placed, it knows not why; it is calmly indifferent
to things, and follows their current. This is the regular
method for guarding the life.

To him who does not dwell in himself the forms of things show themselves as they are. His movement is like that of water (flowing), his stillness is like that of a mirror (showing things just as they are). His tenuity makes him seem to be disappearing altogether; he is still as a clear lake, harmonious in his association with others, and he counts gain as loss. Men all prefer to be first, he alone chooses to be last. Men all choose fullness, he alone chooses emptiness. He does not store, and therefore he has a superabundance; he looks solitary, but has a multitude around him. In his conducting himself he is easy and leisurely and wastes nothing. He does nothing, and laughs at the clever and ingenious.

What is the difference between Qi Gong, and Gung fu?
The truth is that Gung fu and Qi Gung are parts of the same thing such as inhaling and exhaling are part of breathing. In the sense of your question Gung Fu is the external training of the body and the body mechanics where as Qi Gung is the internal training and the cultivation and direction of Qi. The line where one begins and becomes the other is relative. Gung fu training emphasises muscular development and vigorous exercise, Qi Gung emphasises the internal aspects. Shaolin Gung Fu emphasises that:
"if you want your Gung Fu to fly like an eagle you must do Qi Gung, if you want your Qi Gung to fly like an eagle, you must do meditation".
Bruce Eichelberger

The valley spirit never dies.
It is called "the mysterious female."
The opening of the mysterious female
Is called "the root of Heaven and Earth."
Continuous, seeming to remain.

Use it without exertion.

Heaven and Earth last forever.
The reason that Heaven and Earth are able to last forever
Is because they do not give birth to themselves.
Therefore, they are always alive.
Hence, the sage puts herself last and is first.
She is outside herself and therefore her self lasts.

Is it not through her selflessness
That she is able to perfect herself?
The highest goodness is like water.
Water easily benefits all things without struggle.
Yet it abides in places that men hate.
Therefore it is like the Tao.

For dwelling, the Earth is good.
For the mind, depth is good.
The goodness of giving is in the timing.
The goodness of speech is in honesty.
In government, self-mastery is good.
In handling affairs, ability is good.

The Tao is like a great flooding river. How can it be directed to
the left or right? The myriad things rely on it for their life but do
not distinguish it.
It brings to completion but cannot be said to exist.
It clothes and feeds all things without lording over them.

It is always desireless, so we call it "the small."
The myriad things return to it and it doesn't exact lordship
Thus it can be called "great."
Till the end, it does not regard itself as Great.

Therefore it actualizes its greatness.

To accomplish without acting and to obtain without seeking - this
is what is meant by the function of Heaven. Although the Tao of
Heaven is profound, the great man will not deliberate on it,
although it is great, he will not devote his energy to it, although it
is meticulous, he will not scrutinize it. This is what is meant by
refraining from contesting with Heaven.

Chapter Seven:

The Physical
Practice of Tao

The 5,000 year-old concept of the Chinese Five Elemental Phases is an idea that continues its usefulness to this day. Not only do each of the five phases govern various organs of the body, they also give us guiding principles and tangible goals to enable us to live balanced and properly integrated lives.

The Five Elements

Theories of the Five Elements, as outlined below, emerged from an observation of the various groups of dynamic processes, functions and characteristics observed in the natural world.

Water: wet, cool, descending, flowing, yielding
Fire: dry, hot, ascending, moving
Wood: growing, flexible, rooted
Metal: cutting, hard, conducting
Earth: productive, fertile, potential for growth

Each phase or element relates to the others – either supporting, being supported by, controlling or being controlled by them. When an element is unbalanced, difficulties can be caused by either excessive or deficient activity in each phase.

The Five Elements view is important from the perspective of demonstrating the way in which the Chinese system of medicine has built on the Taoist view of balance, process and harmony in the natural world. Developing the information already given in the explanation of *Tai Chi* with its balance of *yin* and *yang*, we give below an expanded table of correspondences:

	Wood	**Fire**	**Earth**	**Metal**	**Water**
Season	Fire	Summer	Late Summer	Autumn	Winter
Direction	East	South	Centre	West	North
Climate	Wind	Heat	Dampness	Dryness	Cold
Colour	Blue/Green	Red	Yellow	White	Blue/Black
Taste	Sour	Bitter	Sweet	Pungent	Salty
Smell	Rancid	Burnt	Fragrant	Rotting	Putrid
Yin Organ (Zang)	Liver	Heart	Spleen	Lungs	Kidney
Yang Organ (Fu)	Gall Bladder	Small Intestine	Stomach	Large Intestine	Bladder
Orifice	Eyes	Tongue	Mouth	Nose	Ears
Tissue	Tendons	Blood Vessels	Muscles	Skin	Bones
Emotion	Anger	Joy	Pensiveness	Grief	Fear
Voice	Shout	Laugh	Sing	Weep	Groan

How Each Phase Works

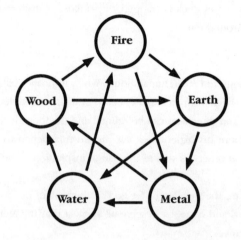

Fire

The element of Fire represents the heart and the *Shen* (Spirit). When properly balanced, Fire manifests open-heartedness, spontaneity, resilience and adaptability. We are able to experience joy, show compassion, and share what we have with others. There is curiosity and a sense of the fullness of life.

A lack of balance shows itself in the inability to give emotionally or to be spontaneous: a person will be too magnanimous – often to the point of self-detriment – and retain no sense of boundary or personal space; there is often lack of joy.

Earth

The Earth element rules the spleen and *Yi* (Mind). Earth, when balanced, highlights the quality of patience, the proper focusing of concentration and the ability to make constructive mental associations; to think 'outside the box'. When the element is present at all times the individual gains stability, security and the good things of life.

When out of balance in the Earth element the individual will show obsessive behaviour, distractedness, experience difficulty in paying attention to the here and now, feel stuck or trapped, or manifest an inability to relate to what is going on around him.

Metal

Metal rules the lungs and *P'o* (Human Soul). When in proper balance, Metal enables us to step back from an experience, to evaluate it and decide on the best action; goals and directions can be refined and the individual is enabled to be objective about his experiences yet remain unattached to outcomes. Respect for self and others as well as the use of inspiration all belong to the Metal element.

Low self-esteem, the inability to let go of others or of the past, chronic grieving or sadness and excessive reserve all suggest that the Metal element may be out of balance.

Water

Water relates to the kidneys and *Zhi* (Will). Maintaining integrity and balance, the individual is able to gather energies and store reserves – the prime function of the Water element. It gives the ability to stay rooted and poised even in the middle of chaotic situations and allows us to set the foundations we require. The element is a strong image in relation to the Tao, for when we are learning to live without preconceived ideas, in a non-judgmental fashion, we must – without fear – allow Life itself to guide us.

When the Water element is out of balance, the individual manifests a lack of direction, has difficulty in completing tasks, demonstrates extreme behaviour and panic, displays a tendency towards fixation on one single course of action.

Wood

The element of Wood rules the liver and *Hun* (the Heavenly Soul). Balance in this element is expressed by the ability to transcend limitations – both personal and external. Just as a living tree can break down an obstacle, or grow despite its surroundings so we can transcend difficulties. Focusing one's purpose, setting goals, doing the best one can and breaking new ground all belong to this phase.

Negative manifestations of imbalances with this element are depression, lack of courage and purpose, impulsiveness, anger, irritability and frustration or – conversely – being overly cautious, unwilling to take risks and being unable to get out of a rut.

How The Phases Interact

Looking at the previous diagram and working in a clockwise direction, it can be seen that each element is supported by the one immediately before it, supports the one immediately after it, controls the second element after it in a clockwise direction and is controlled by the third element.
As an example:

Fire is supported by Wood

Wood supports Earth

Earth is controlled by Water

Water controls Metal

Thus an act of spontaneity receives energy from the ability to overcome boundaries, is able to give proper attention to the task in hand, but does not take on too much at a time so that there is an opportunity to evaluate what needs to be done in the light of previous experience.

The example above demonstrates the principle of interaction in terms of self-awareness. The principle, however, has multiple applications in the world in which we live and it is relatively easy to see how this works if we think in terms of natural cycles.

The Sheng Cycle – Support and Promotion

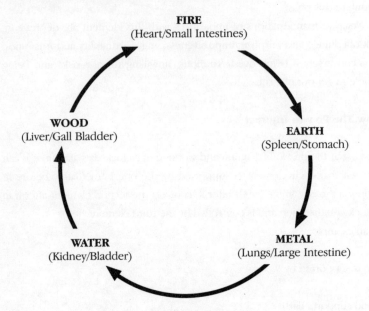

FIRE
(Heart/Small Intestines)

WOOD
(Liver/Gall Bladder)

EARTH
(Spleen/Stomach)

WATER
(Kidney/Bladder)

METAL
(Lungs/Large Intestine)

This cycle represents the manner in which the elements – and organ systems of the body – support and promote one another: Fire burns to create Earth, Water nourishes the growth of Wood, and so on. When this theory is applied to Chinese medicine similar relationships develop; the Heart supports the Spleen, the Spleen supports the Lungs and so on.

This inter-relationship is sometimes referred to as the 'Mother and Son' cycle in the sense of dependencies. For example, the Kidney would be 'mother' to her 'son' the Liver. An example of this is when the Kidney Yin is deficient, which often leads to the deficiency of Liver Yin energy, and the 'mother' can be used to treat her 'son'. Another instance of this would be that if the Lung energy were deficient, it could be treated by toning the Spleen.

The Ke Cycle – The Cycle of Mutual Control

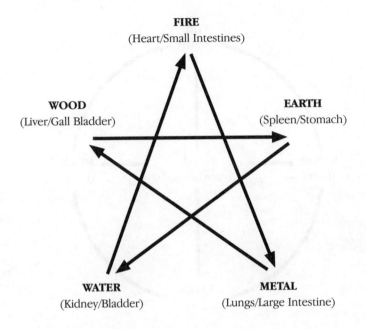

FIRE
(Heart/Small Intestines)

WOOD
(Liver/Gall Bladder)

EARTH
(Spleen/Stomach)

WATER
(Kidney/Bladder)

METAL
(Lungs/Large Intestine)

This set of relationships refers to the manner in which the Elements in the natural world are seen to control each other as part of the process of dynamic balance. Fire will 'control' Metal in the sense that Fire will melt Metal, while Water will 'control' Fire. In Chinese medicine the notion of control is seen as part of the process of one organ assisting another. When disharmony occurs, a weak organ may be unable to exert the control and assistance needed by another.

If the Lung energy is weak there may be a tendency for the Liver energy to be uncontrolled and to rise. This may manifest itself in headaches or high blood pressure. If the Spleen is overly 'damp' – that is, the bodily system is somewhat waterlogged – it may inhibit the Liver's ability to move energy around the body.

The Cosmological Sequence – Mirror of the Human Body

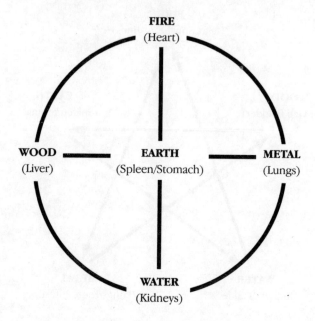

FIRE
(Heart)

WOOD   EARTH   METAL
(Liver)   (Spleen/Stomach)   (Lungs)

WATER
(Kidneys)

The third sequence that arises from the Five Elements view, which has it roots in the Taoist nature view as well as Chinese numerology, is known as the Cosmological Sequence. This sequence places the Water Element at the root and thus at the cycle's most important point.

As the Water Element corresponds to the Kidneys this points to the importance in Chinese medicine of the Kidneys. They are viewed as the root of the *yin* and *yang* energy in the body and therefore by implication in all the other organs.

The Spleen, which is placed at the centre of the Cosmological Sequence, is seen as the origin of *chi* (energy or breath) in the body and as such the focus of support for all the other organs.

Causes of Disharmony

Chinese medicine is more holistic than Western systems, believing that the internal organs have an effect not only on the physical functions of the body but also the psychological and spiritual aspects. The major causes of disharmony are considered to be psychological in nature and are termed the 'seven emotions'. These seven emotions are Anger, Joy, Sadness, Grief, Pensiveness, Fear and Fright. Chinese medicine does not categorize emotions in any rigid fashion, and overlaps are not considered to present any particular difficulty. In some instances, there are clearly common characteristics between several of these emotions and it is the scale of emotion which is quantifiable with certain pairs – for example, Sadness and Grief, Fear and Fright.

There is another form of classification: *zang* and *fu* are differentiated by the varying features of their functions. The five *zang* organs mainly manufacture and store essence (*chi*), blood and body fluids. The six *fu* organs mainly receive and digest food, absorb nutrient substances, transmit and excrete wastes. The five *zang* organs store up essential *chi* and regulate its outflow. The six *fu* organs transform and transport substances without storing them. For this reason they may become too full to be used effectively although they cannot be filled to capacity. The *zang-fu* organs also have *yin* and *yang* aspects, the six *fu* organs are considered *yang* while the *zang* organs are *yin*. Each of the *zang-fu* organs itself can again be further subdivided into *yin* or *yang* functions.

In the Five Elements system the emotions can be associated with the bodily organ system as shown below.

EMOTION	ZANG	FU
Anger	Liver	Gall Bladder
Joy	Heart	Small Intestine
Sadness, Grief	Lungs	Large Intestine
Pensiveness	Spleen	Stomach
Fear, Fright	Kidney	Bladder

The seven emotions are considered neither good nor bad; it is how they are balanced that is important. Too much Joy is as imbalanced as too much Grief; the disharmony will simply manifest itself differently.

Patterns of Disharmony

In Chinese medicine the diagnostic process is conducted in four areas – the four examinations. They are: looking, hearing and smelling, questioning, touching. There are also several different organizational patterns that can be applied. The most commonly used in primary diagnosis are the Eight Principles, and these are often determined by the colour and condition of the tongue. These Eight Principles are groups of symptoms resulting in very clear patterns.

External Pattern
Symptoms: acute illness with sudden onset of fever and chills; body aches; headache; aversion to wind, cold and/or heat.
Condition of tongue: normal, thin coat.

Internal Pattern
Symptoms: chronic conditions; internal organ dysfunction; pain and discomfort in trunk; digestive disorders; changes in stool and urine; fever with no chills or dislike of cold.
Condition of tongue: changes in tongue colour and coat.

Excess Pattern
Symptoms: ponderous, heavy movement; heavy, coarse perspiration; pressure and touch increase discomfort.
Condition of tongue: thick coating.

Deficiency Pattern
Symptoms: frail, weak movement; tiredness and fatigue; shortness of breath;

pressure relieves discomfort; inactive, passive appearance; low voice; little appetite; dizziness.

Condition of tongue: pale colour, thin coat.

Heat Pattern

Symptoms: red face; fever; sensation of heat; dislike of heat; cold reduces discomfort; rapid movements; outgoing manner; thirst or desire for cold drinks; dark urine; constipation.

Condition of tongue: red colour, yellow coat.

Cold Pattern

Symptoms: pale, white face; cold limbs; fear of cold; heat reduces discomfort; slow movements; withdrawn manner; no thirst or a desire for hot drinks; clear urine; watery stools.

Condition of tongue: pale colour, white coat.

Yang Pattern

Symptoms: red face; fever; hot feeling; agitated and active manner; dry mouth; thirst; constipation with bad smell; dark urine; full pulse.

Condition of tongue: bright red and scarlet tongue or yellow and black coating.

Yin Pattern

Symptoms: pale face; low spirit; feels cold; cold limbs; tired and weak; low voice; reduced appetite; no taste in mouth; little thirst; copious and clear urine; slow and sinking; weak; frail pulse.

Condition of tongue: pale and swollen.

The Eight Principles are used by applying the information gained to the *zang-fu* system, the Five Elements and – especially with relatively simple external conditions – the channel or Meridian lines of power within the body. A holistic and accurate picture of imbalance and disharmony can thus be drawn up.

Chapter Seven

Effective Use

When working with others, the Five Phases may be used as a basis for evaluating personality traits and tendencies. The most important question regarding this way of operating is how best to use the information gained. The Five Phases form such an integral part of Chinese life that they can be used for everything from planting crops to family interactions to running governments and businesses. In the context of a complete holistic treatment, appropriate counterbalancing and supporting affirmations might be given, or suggestions made to the patient to enhance, at the level of the patient's beliefs, the idea of total balance.

The concept of the Five Phases can be most effectively used as a basis for meditation or be incorporated into other energy balancing exercises. This helps to ground them within the individual to the point where the intuitive balancing becomes second nature. Ultimately though we have to move beyond the concept.

> The five colours blind the eye
> The five tones deafen the ear
> The five flavours dull the taste.
> Racing and hunting madden the mind.
> Precious things lead one astray
>
> Therefore the sage is guided by what he feels and not by what he sees
> He lets go of that and chooses this.

When studying and living by the Tao we have to remember that Tao itself is the regulator of the rhythms and balances of Nature. It is 'always without action but nevertheless brings about everything'. So in understanding the drive for health and healing, the Taoist looks for help which is natural in its origin. It seems that some passages of the *Tao Te Ching* refer to already-known longevity practices that were being used in certain circles even at the time of its writing.

All the ancient techniques – *Tai Chi Chuan*, *Chi Gung* and others – were geared towards preserving the life spark in such a way that each individual could maintain the suppleness and energy of the very young, thus enabling them to live the longest possible life.

Holiness and wisdom were, and are, a natural result of the powerful vitality that manifests itself when one takes control of the vital energy. Whatever could be done to enhance the vital energy led the individual nearer and nearer to becoming a sage or Holy man able to become immortal and therefore transcendent.

Lao Tse admonishes the seeker of the Way and suggests that the ultimate goal is to embrace Unity and to develop the 'inner light'. Since he also suggests that becoming like the 'mysterious feminine' (*yin*) within is an important part of this practice, we can accept that this – in part – signifies the potential to access the ability to achieve peace and tranquillity. Lao Tse is not terribly precise as to the mystical experiences he refers to since such events are always highly individual. Chuang Tse is somewhat more open and gives a better idea of the ways in which Unity can be reached.

One way of achieving mystical union is continence in sexual behaviour. *Ching* literally denotes the semen of a man or the menstrual flow of a woman and therefore is 'seed essence'. In Taoist texts, however, it describes a subtle substance or essence, capable of combining with *chi* (vital energy). Taoist adepts try to resist the loss of *ching* by means of various sexual practices and techniques (*fang-chung shu*, *huan-ching pu-nao*) which, like tantric yoga, are essentially based on avoiding ejaculation and strengthening the *ching* with the help of the female *yin* essence. Any illnesses are healed and the life force is thus increased. Ideally, rather than ejaculating, the adept should be able to allow the energy of the semen to return to nourish the brain (*huan-ching pu-nao*).

The adept in the Taoist arts put almost immeasurable emphasis on cultivating the energy of the Three Treasures – *Ching*, *Chi* and *Shen*. When these are interacting harmoniously, we live life at peak capacity. Our body, mind and spirit are fully engaged in the business of life, and everything simply seems to click into place.

Chapter Seven

We have to learn the various techniques for developing, managing, expanding and utilizing the Three Treasures. Along with the exercise systems and acupressure, diet and, perhaps most powerfully of all, the type of herbalism sometimes known as tonic herbalism, are all aspects of care which have to do with what we put into our bodies.

Chinese Herbalism

Herbal preparations have long been used in China and there is evidence of a shamanic culture from as far back as 2000 BC, that used plant, mineral and animal substances to treat ailments.

The history of Chinese medicine *per se* dates back to Shen Nung, born over 5,400 years ago. Known as the father of agriculture, and probably of civilization itself, he is said to have recorded the great herbal text '*Shen Nung Pan Tsao*'. He also taught people how to raise crops, identify various therapeutic herbs and rear domestic animals.

Next in importance are the writings of the Yellow Emperor's Inner Classic (*Huang Di Nei Jing*). These are recorded in the form of a dialogue between the Yellow Emperor (2697–2597 BC) and his physician Qi Bo. In it they talk about the whole gamut of Chinese medicine – acupuncture, cause of disease, diagnosis, the Five Elements, pathology and Yin Yang. Over the succeeding centuries the use of therapeutic substances was refined and developed: by about AD 659 a comprehensive '*materia medica*' was beginning to emerge, which listed the herbal components and described their actions and properties.

Herbs tend to be highly clear-cut in their actions and many of the formulae used in Taoist medicine – which makes use of what is around us in the natural world – contain a range of herbs that not only possess different qualities and properties but also target different aspects of the patient's disharmony. Modern Western Taoists often study the applications of herbs that are more readily available to them than those which are peculiarly Chinese. Treating the body holistically shows that changes in the individual on any level (physical, mental or spiritual) will have an effect on all of the systems.

A shift in the physical condition changes the way you think and feel – pain being the most obvious example of this – and affects the intuitive and emotional reactions. When the mind is brought into the equation it can, both directly and indirectly, influence overall and subtle changes in our physical nature and in the actions we take. Taoist herbalism aims to address the total picture, so it is possible for certain herbs to work on several different functions at the same time. Overall, the practitioner has to weigh up a number of factors when preparing a formula, for the notion of the unity of the body and psyche is absolutely central to the Oriental healing arts.

The goal of Taoist herbalism is, therefore, to allow the body–mind connection to maintain its self-regulatory capacity, resulting in a new awareness of well-being, and a new level of health and happiness that can form the foundation for a creative, successful life. Ultimately, in line with the Taoists of old, it will bring about true spiritual discovery and growth and, hopefully, eventual mastery and enlightenment.

The most important aspect of the tonic herbs that are often used lies in what is now known as their 'adaptogenic' quality rather than their curative function. This is the ability to enhance each individual's capacity to adapt to changes, both in their circumstances and in the environment around them. The greater the stresses of life and the more dynamic the changes in one's life, the greater is the requirement for adaptive energy. This perhaps explains the increased interest in Oriental herbalism in the West as life has become more and more frenetic.

Shen is best translated as the spirit or higher self. Certain *shen* tonics encourage the opening up of the higher self. There are also *shen* 'stabilizers' which help regulate our emotions so that we can take advantage of this access to our higher self and thus act within Tao. This allows us to have access to our complete emotional selves, but our emotions are allowed free expression without the process dominating our lives or becoming obsessive or addictive. *Shen* tonics have been used throughout history by the great sages of the Orient to help in their quest for enlightenment and harmony with God, nature and all of mankind.

Properties of Herbs

Herbs in Taoist medicine can be considered in terms of several classifications:

The Four Energies

The four essential energy qualities of herbs relate to their associated temperatures: herbs are selected to balance conditions with opposite characteristics. Since *yin* is cooling, moistening and relaxing, *yin* deficiency is often characterized by hot conditions, feelings of heat, dryness and agitation. *Yang*, on the other hand, is warming, drying and invigorating. Therefore *yang* deficiency is characterized by cold feelings and conditions, excessive moistness and a lack of vitality (fatigue).

Cool or cold herbs relieve conditions where there is Heat in the body whilst warm or hot herbs relieve Cold symptoms. Some herbs are neither hot nor cold, and in essence they describe a fifth energy, that of natural herbs. For example, Sheng Di Huang (fresh Chinese foxglove root) is a cool/cold herb which relieves Heat; Rou Gui (cinnamon bark) is a warm/hot herb which relieves Cold symptoms; Fu Ling (poria) is a neutral herb.

The Five Tastes

We saw earlier how the Five Elements give rise to the methods of classification in Chinese medicine. The five taste qualities of herbs relate to their action on the *chi* of the body and therefore describe the therapeutic effect of herbs; the five tastes are sour, bitter, pungent, sweet and salty.

Sour is astringent and herbs in this category consolidate *chi* and secretions, nourishing the Liver and Gallbladder, controlling the function of the *zang-fu* system. Bitter Herbs are drying, detoxifying and antibiotic; they drain *chi* downwards, reducing excess and they strengthen the Heart and Small Intestine. Sweet herbs act as a tonic, by nourishing and relaxing the body and slowing *chi* down; they harmonize the Spleen and Stomach, nourishing the blood. Pungent herbs stimulate, warm and raise *chi* from the interior to the exterior. Pungent herbs strengthen the Lungs and Large Intestine and invigorate the Blood. Salty herbs soften lumps and blockages and assist with the flow of *chi*, strengthening the Kidney and Bladder in the process. Some herbs, described as bland, are relatively neutral in terms of taste and might be used to alter the degree of action of another herb.

In Taoist herbal medicine, individual herbs are thought to enter specific channels or meridians, thereby being directed towards the system of balance associated with that channel. In reality, the energy of specific herbs influences particular *zang-fu* systems. For example, when it is said that the herb Da Zao (the Chinese date) enters the Spleen and Stomach channels, its energy is used by herbalists to tonify the Spleen and augment the *chi*.

As Chinese medicine becomes more available in the West, more people are undertaking studies which show the naturalness and efficacy of the cures. For those brought up in western traditions it can be a little difficult to become accustomed to having to boil up ones' own medication. Once however the natural distaste has been overcome the benefits soon become apparent, Nowadays the herbs are often presented differently anyway.

Below is a brief table showing how herbs are matched with symptoms. Both conventional and Chinese names are given. Please note, however, that the table does not suggest how the herbs may be combined, since this decision can only be taken by the practitioner after an extensive consultation.

Nature of Disharmony	Herb	Action
Chi deficiency	Dang Shen (Codonopsis root)	*Chi* tonic
Blood deficiency	He Shou Wu (Polygonum root)	Blood tonic
Yang deficiency	Du Zhong (Eucommia bark)	*Yang* tonic
Yin deficiency	Mai Men Dong (Liriope root tuber)	*Yin* tonic
Stagnant *Chi*	Chen Pi (Citrus rind)	regulates *Chi*
Stagnant Blood	Chuan Xiong (Ligusticum root)	invigorates Blood
Interior Cold	Rou Gui (Cinnamomum bark)	warms and expels Cold
Interior Heat/toxicity	Tu Fu Ling (Smilacis rhizome)	clears Heat and toxins
Exterior invasion (Cold)	Gui Zhi (Cinnamomum stems)	expels/disperses Cold
Exterior invasion (Heat)	Chai Hu (Bupleurum root)	expels/disperses Heat
Extreme interior Heat	Shi Gao (Gypsum)	drains Fire/Heat
Interior Damp	Cang Zhu (Atractylodes root)	transforms damp
Disturbed *Shen* (spirit)	Suan Zao Ren (Ziziphus seeds)	calms *Shen*

The classification of herbal qualities into energies and tastes shows what each herb can do. However, these qualities are not fixed; they all exist on a scale. A herb may be slightly warm, warm, very warm, hot and so on, and possess other qualities of energy and taste. How one prepares the herb also has an effect on the way it acts. For example, frying a herb encourages its energy to move upwards and outwards whereas preparing a herb with salt promotes a descending flowing action.

It is worthwhile noting that while herbs are prescribed for certain ailments, knowledge of the qualities and action of herbs can become an integral part of every Taoist practitioner's armoury – part and parcel of their search for their own Tao – and can be used every day in the construction of diets geared to maximum health.

Diet

In order to apply the principles of Tao to your eating habits, you need to keep three maxims in mind.

1. *Moderation*. Eat according to your individual appetite at regular times throughout the day so that digestion is complete before you sleep. Your total intake should be enough to make you feel comfortable but not full.

2. *Discipline*. Use fresh seasonal organic produce in the correct proportions for your appetite, obtained locally wherever feasible. Prepare, serve and eat food in an attentive, respectful way.

3. *Balance*. Be aware of the need for energetic balance according to the five flavours – sweet, sour, salty, bitter, pungent – when preparing and combining foods.

You need to eat when you are hungry and drink when you are thirsty; don't attempt to eat if you are upset or emotional. This supports the four energies in the most appropriate way.

It is often said that the act of digestion is a form of internal cooking designed to release the energy held in the food, thereby making it able to support our life force. For this reason the food that we eat should be cooked lightly, avoiding heavy fats, and eaten warm. Preferably it should not be microwaved or over-spiced, since this upsets the energy balance. Too much cold raw food can also upset the internal balance as can overly sweet food and excess animal protein. Over-processing of food and poor preparation may well be at the root of many Western ailments.

In many ways the Taoist principle of emptiness can be applied to dietary matters, since the empty kitchen would signify that only enough food is brought in for present needs and is cooked just enough to allow it to be easily assimilated by the body. This is adopting a very simple approach.

The adept will often use diet to prepare himself for meditative and alchemical practices which help him communicate with the cosmos. In China, alchemy is a doctrine designed to help the practitioner understand how the cosmos works. Just as in the West, various processes of refinement of base material are carried out in order to discover the essence or inner quality of each substance and, more interestingly, each procedure. As he makes his discoveries the practitioner overcomes the limits of his own individuality and achieves the status of Perfect Man.

Alchemy

Chinese alchemy was subjected to some fairly radical developments over time. Not least was its division into two principal traditions at around the beginning of the Tang period (AD 618–907). These traditions were *waidan* or 'external alchemy' and *neidan* or 'internal alchemy.' The latter developed as an independent discipline but owes its terms and techniques to the former. The study of alchemy in China once more attracted popular interest after 1926 when the *Tao Tsang* (Taoist Canon) was reprinted and made widely available. The majority of Chinese alchemical sources are found in the Canon, though texts later than the fifteenth century are included in the Essentials of the Taoist Canon and in minor collections.

Alchemy in China has always been closely related to the teachings that are found in the early philosophical texts of Taoism, especially the *Lao Tse* and the *Chuang Tse* Scriptures. When alchemists accept the apparent separation of 'Primeval Unity' into the two complementary principles of *yin* and *yang*, their task becomes the retracing of the process of this division to its source. The idea is that alchemy – both 'external' and 'internal' – gives the adept enough information and technique to enable him to understand the secrets of Tao. The two processes are mirrors of one another and can only be learned through the good offices and oral instruction (*koujue*) of a Master, who is the judge of how much knowledge a pupil can handle. The spontaneous appreciation of what he is taught is an important part of the learning process, since it is thought to create an elixir of life within the alchemist himself.

In order to transcend space and time and gain access to timelessness, or 'immortality', the alchemist must ensure that space and time work together in harmony at the exact moment at which he performs the actions that bring about the changes he requires. His sacred space is actually a point which has no dimension (like a charmed circle) and has to be protected by the talismans he uses (*fu*), and by the chamber of the elixirs (*danwu*) which is the laboratory itself. His tools and instruments must be properly calibrated and oriented according to the Elements or Five Phases so that he can safely step up the rhythms of Nature and achieve the sequences pertinent to the task in hand in the shortest possible time. The idea is that from that point of emptiness – no-thingness – the true adept is able to move freely along the continuum that connects the higher and lower levels of existence, the *tian* and the *yuan*.

There are two principal procedures in alchemy, the first being the amalgamation of lead and mercury. In external alchemy this compound is thought to resemble Primeval Unity in its energy properties. The next, equally important, method involves cinnabar. Cinnabar is naturally occurring mercury sulphide, and when the mercury (which we now know to be highly toxic) that is contained within cinnabar is extracted and added to fresh sulphur, certain changes occur: an elixir that was thought to be similar in vibration to the luminescence of Pure Energy is the result. This luminescent energy represents the One before its separation into the two complementary principles of *yin* and *yang*. In alchemical experiments the process of refining takes place in nine consecutive stages, a process rather similar to that of the dilution and succussion (shaking) that is performed in homeopathy. Each cycle of refinement yields a 'gold' that can be consumed by the alchemist, or used as an ingredient in the next cycle.

Huandan (the Elixir of Return) originally signified an elixir obtained by bringing the ingredients back to their original condition. In internal alchemy, lead represents the knowledge of the Tao with which each individual is blessed, but which must be revealed by the application of the individual mind, symbolized by mercury. In internal alchemy, the adept's own being performs the function that natural substances and instruments play in external alchemy, and a transmutation of energy takes place. *Jindan* (the Golden Elixir) is also the name of the art of alchemy.

The Tang period marked the transition to internal alchemy. The *Shangqing* (Supreme Purity) tradition of Taoism paid particular attention to meditation, but also taught the compounding of elixirs. Possibly because the substances used were so toxic and, when not used with the correct knowledge, defeated rather than enhanced the search for longevity, a way was needed which brought about the transmutation of energy within the individual. The discipline of self-management was therefore of supreme importance. If the adept were sufficiently successful in his *neidan* he would become a being of light and therefore immortal.

Both the Southern Lineage (*nanzong*) and Northern Lineage (*beizong*) schools encouraged the cultivation of *xing* (one's original nature) and *ming* (the given life energy), because they were seen as the two main constituents of *neidan*. Briefly, *xing* is pure being and non-being (essence) and *ming* is how one expresses that (or not, as the case may be) in life. Various schools laid a greater or lesser emphasis on each aspect. The eighteenth century witnessed an increased interest in a much more spiritual interpretation of the whole idea of longevity, the attainment of immortality and the transmutation of internal energies. Spiritual immortality implies not only freedom from life and death but also from the problems of time, space and sexual identity – although immortals are often depicted as either male or female. The practice of allowing semen (*ching*) to return to nourish the brain (*huan-ching pu-nao*) is considered to be highly desirable. Taoist practice incorporates several methods that achieve this balance.

Originally, alchemical instruction and the use of elixirs was said to have been communicated directly from Heaven to the Yellow Emperor. The *Book of the Nine Elixirs* is reputed to be the earthly version of a scripture kept in Heaven and conveyed from divinity to divinity. Before it was transmitted in a form understandable to human beings, it was known as the 'Superior Book of the Nine Methods of the Noble Lady of the Primordial Dao of the Nine Heavens' (*Jiutian Yuandao jun jiuding zhi shangjing*). The Yellow Emperor, Huangdi, (the legendary first ancestor of the Chinese nation) does not seem to have been a master, but he is represented as having received teachings from such divinities as the Mysterious Woman, the Pure Woman (*Su-nü*), Guangcheng zi, or Qi Bo.

The Mysterious Woman and Pure Woman may be taken as aspects of *yin* energy, so the knowledge was either of an inspirational nature or was a direct transmission from Pure Yin or *K'un*, (the Great Mother). The number nine in Chinese numerology is the Fire element, so alchemy is, in that sense, the transmission of fire and an understanding of its transmutation into its very essence. This leads us very neatly back to the reasons for the *weidan* (external) work with cinnabar and the search for an elixir which would reveal the secrets of the Tao and of immortality.

Becoming Immortal

We have seen that Taoist adepts continually endeavoured to achieve 'immortality'. This ultimately meant that they could transcend death itself: as preparation for that they trained themselves to achieve a state of ecstasy. Achieving this state indicates that adepts are able to make their entire being become one with the totality of the Ultimate. Viewed by others when they are in that state, it appears that the life spark has left the body and has gone back to 'the beginning of things', as Chuang Tse called it. In fact, from a purely subjective viewpoint, adepts have the ability to fly off and move about without restraint in their own inner space. This phenomenon is, of course, similar to what we now call astral travel and to the shamanic journey as understood by the North American Indians.

This state of mystical ecstasy is by no means permanent, nor can every adept achieve it. More important is the journey (the Way) towards absolute freedom that adepts undertake as they learn to live in harmony with all the cosmic forces. Chuang Tse uses the theme of a voyage to demonstrate how adepts can best align themselves with these forces and show how they cease to be in conflict with them, while at the same time living within the Tao and through it. They thus become Perfected Man.

The adept would not necessarily choose to withdraw from the world, but is simultaneously able to live as an ordinary man among others and yet live free of worldly attachments. He would, in modern day parlance, 'walk his talk'. For the Chinese who strove to balance the inner and outer states the master could be internally a saint and externally a ruler but, according to Lao Tse, had no need or wish to parade his influence in front of others. He was simply aware of the power that he had.

Many Taoist scriptures describe *hsien-jen* (the Immortals) as beings so fully immersed in the universal life that they could perform the magical acts of the true adept – they could transform themselves at will into whatever they pleased and could manifest and multiply themselves, or even become invisible. In Western terms they were shape-shifters and stories about them were in existence before Taoism became popular. Chuang Tse describes, in quite a lyrical fashion, the immortals whom he calls divine men in touch with the Ultimate.

These divine men, who dwelt on a mountain known as *K'un-lun*, did not eat cereals such as wheat, but fed on the wind and dew (hence *feng shui* – wind and water). It was also said they could operate in the air, borne aloft by the clouds or flying dragons. Nowadays we would again recognize these qualities as belonging to the shamanic traditions. The *Shan-hai ching* scripture speaks of men resembling the immortals whose bodies were covered with feathers. The commentary to the text states that they were capable of flying like birds. This again is perhaps an aspect of shamanic practice, for shamans believed that they could take on the qualities of the animals and birds whose skins they wore. Operating within the Tao conferred the use of magical powers on the adept.

When the adept came to the realization that physical death was approaching he announced to his followers that he was about to disappear: he would then put himself into an altered state of consciousness where it would appear that – as with the ecstatic trance – he had departed this life. Following a ritual burial, the casket was reopened, when there would be found a stick, a sword, or a sandal depending on the adept's degree of mysticism. This process, whereby the physical body was transmuted into something which could not be destroyed, was known as *shih-chieh*. There were many levels of *shih-chieh*, but the one most revered was the 'great accomplishment' when, as the result of truly alchemical practices, the *atavar* (holy one) would rise up in full daylight to the heavens as a body of light. Here we might contemplate on the meaning of the resurrection of Christ, which occurred in a similar manner.

In ancient Chinese mythology, the Immortals went to live in Heavenly Realms. The realms most often evoked in Taoist literature are the Isles of the Blessed. These islands could not be approached by mere mortals and would disappear under the waves if one did not possess the correct knowledge to access them. Here, in the East, was found a natural drug that was said to prevent one from dying. Later, theologians perceived that the heavens mirrored the Imperial Court, with a structure administered by differing grades of celestial servants. The destiny of Immortals was to occupy a position in this hierarchy, although if they transgressed they could be demoted, even to the point of having to reincarnate and begin again in the physical realms.

For the Taoists, while *K'un-Lun* is an actual physical mountain range in Western China, it was also a path leading to Heaven. Whoever manages to climb to the top of *K'un-Lun* gains access to the heavens for it is the place 'where the ten thousand things have their origin and where alternate the yin and the yang'. It is that space between heaven and earth wherein resides true spiritual power and the right to true immortality.

In his search for longevity, the Taoist practitioner also searched deep in the mountains for the vegetable and mineral substances he needed. This was alien country to him and he had to protect himself from all kinds of dangers. The use of talismans and magical formulae thus became an integral part of the adept's knowledge and he would travel from mountain to mountain in the hope of encountering a master who would initiate him in the knowledge he sought. Within what was thought of as the womb of the earth, ancient heroes had hidden the principles of life – elixirs and sacred scriptures – and these places, illuminated sometimes from within by their own light or externally through an opening that let in a luminous ray from Heaven, were considered sacred. Physical immortality was achieved by the use of the various plants that were encountered, some of which are found in Chinese medicine today. Also utilised was the water of the River of Cinnabar that was crossed on the journey. (Cinnabar is actually mercury sulphide and was often thought to be the blood of the Dragon, a magical substance.)

K'un-Lun is also perceived as a pagoda representing the stages the individual had to ascend in order to be admitted into the spiritual hierarchy and reach the Ultimate, rather akin to the chakras in Buddhist thought. However, *K'un-Lun* was primarily known as the abode of Hsi Wang-Mu, Queen Mother of the West. She became the Queen of the Immortals, who, it was believed, cavorted on this mountain, riding dragons and geese. In her original guise of tiger-woman she brought the plague to China, but later became a more benign goddess. She is portrayed as a young beautiful woman wearing a royal gown, sometimes riding a peacock. Her favourite animal is Feng-huang, the Chinese phoenix which is the personification of the primordial force of the heavens and the symbol of immortality. Feng-huang has the head and the comb of a pheasant and the tail of a peacock.

Legend has it that Hsi Wang-Mu's jade palace lies near the Lake of Jewels, surrounded by a golden wall over a thousand miles long. In her garden grows the Peach of Immortality which forms only once every three thousand years, taking another three thousand years to ripen. When it is ripe, Hsi Wang-Mu invites the other Immortals who live on the mountain, segregated by gender, to a feast in celebration of the event and to eat the miraculous peach, which bestows on them yet another period of immortality. This is *Ch'ang-sheng pu-ssu*.

Eight Immortals of Chinese Mythology

As a group, the principal Eight Immortals symbolize Taoism, transmutation and happiness. They are extremely popular folk heroes in Chinese culture. They travel through the ages in each other's company, instructing the worthy and helping the needy.

Li T'ieh-kuai or Li Tie Guai

Taught to be an immortal by Hsi Wang-Mu, Queen of the Immortals, 'Iron-crutch Li' always carries a crutch and a gourd in which he keeps medicine to help people. Some say that the gourd contains the elixir of life made from the Peaches of Immortality that grow in Hsi Wang-Mu's garden.

Chungli Ch'uan or Zhongli Quan

Usually shown with a fan, he represents the military man. In his old age he became a hermit and lived on Yang-chiu Mountain in Shansi where he learned to become an immortal. He was said to have been carried by a stork into the Heavens.

Lan Ts'ai-ho or Lan Cai He

The strolling singer, depicted as either a woman or a young boy and shown with a flower-basket or a flute – the symbol of harmony – she is the patron deity of florists and of horticulture.

Chang Kuo-lao or Zhang Guo lao

Said to have lived in the seventh or early eighth century, he was once the head of the Imperial Academy. Usually depicted riding his magic mule, facing its tail and carrying a bamboo-tube drum with iron sticks, he is the emblem of old men. The mule is said to have been able to travel thousands of miles a day and would turn to paper on reaching its destination, to be pocketed by the deity.

Ho Hsien-ku or He XianGu

A woman, the Female Sage, she is said to have lived in the late seventh century, often shown with a lotus blossom or flower basket, and occasionally with a peach and sheng reed-organ. Directed in a dream to grind up a stone called Yun-mu and eat it, she did so, vowing chastity at the same time. Summoned to the Imperial Court she disappeared en route. She is a patron deity of women, particularly housewives.

Lu Tung-pin or Lu Dong Bin

Born c. AD 755 and died AD 805, he is shown with a fly-whisk. Dressed as a scholar he is honoured as such: after his death became venerated as the King of Medicine. He had a magic sword with which he performed bizarre actions; he is also the patron deity of barbers. He represents wealth and literacy.

Han Hsiang-tzu or Han Xiang Zi

Said to be the nephew of the Tang Dynasty statesman and scholar Han Yu, he is often shown with a flute and is the patron deity of musicians. He became an immortal by eating one of the Peaches of Immortality. He carries with him a basket of fruit or flowers. He was a disciple of Lu Tung-pin.

Ts'ao Kuo-ch'iu or Cao Guo Jiu

He is said to have been connected with the Sung Imperial family, and is generally shown with castanets or a jade tablet which offers admission to court. He is the patron deity of actors.

THOUGHTS AND IDEAS

As this chapter is all about staying alive, working with your own nature,
understanding the five elements, and ultimately reaching 'immortality'
the quotes I have chosen reflect this. They are about being 'happy in
one's own skin' and living with the idea that we are responsible for our
own environment and well-being.

Pursue the Tao of Nature
There's a limit to life, but to knowledge there's no limit. Using
what's limited to seek out the unlimited is futile.
And if, knowing this, we still act according to knowledge,
then danger can't be avoided.
Don't do good for the sake of gain, and if you pursue evil
then try not to get punished. To be in accord with the Tao of
your own nature is the regular way to preserve your body,
to maintain life, to nourish your inner core,
and to live out your years.
What is this Tao of our own nature?

Spiritual Teachings of the Tao by Mark Forstater

Law of Gravity
The Law of Gravity .....
Falling free
Falling free....the root of lightness

Repose....is the root of movement
Stillness.....the master of agitation

Gravity is.......Falling free
Timothy Leary
Psychedelic Prayers

The sage never thinks of Heaven nor men. He does not think of taking the initiative, nor of anything external to himself. He moves along with his age, and does not vary or fail. Amid all the completeness of his doings, he is never exhausted.

Chuang Tse was fishing in the River Pu when the King of Chu sent two officers to convey this message: 'I wish to trouble you with the administration of all my lands.'
Chuang Tse kept holding his rod and without looking round said, 'I understand that in Chu there's a sacred tor-toise shell, 3,000 years old, which the King keeps in his ancestral temple, covered with a rich cloth. Do you think it was better for the tortoise to die, and leave its shell to be honoured in this way, or would it have been better to be alive, dragging its tail through the mud?'
One of the officers said, 'It would be better for it to live.'
Chuang Tse nodded and said, 'Then go away. I'll keep on dragging my tail after me through the mud.'

Tseng Tse lived in Wei. He wore an old robe quilted with hemp, whose outer layer was missing. His face looked worn and emaciated and his hands and feet were hard and cal-lused. He often lived for three days without lighting a fire and ten years between new clothes. If he tried to put his cap on straight, the straps would break; if he tightened the lapels of his robe, his elbows would poke through; when he put on his shoes, the heels would separate at the back.

Yet, dragging his shoes along, he sang the Hymns of Shang with a voice that filled Heaven and Earth as if it came from a bronze bell or a stone chime. The King couldn't convince him to be a minister and no feudal prince could make him their friend.

So it is that one who nourishes the soul forgets the body, one who nourishes the physical form forgets all thoughts of gain, and one who carries out the Tao forgets all about the mind.

By length of time one acquires ability at any art; and how much more one who is ever at work on it!

Duke Huan was hunting in a marsh with Guan Zhong as his carriage driver, when he saw a ghost. The duke grasped Guan Zhong's hand and said "Father Zhong what do you see?

"I don't see anything," replied Guan Zhong.

When the duke returned home, he fell into a stupor, grew ill, and for several days did not go out.

A gentleman of Qi named Huangzi Gaoao said, "Your Grace, you are doing this injury to yourself How could a ghost have the power to injure you! If the vital breath that is stored up in a man becomes dispersed and does not return, then he suffers a deficiency. If it ascends and fails to descend again, it causes him to be chronically irritable. If it descends and does not ascend again, it causes him to be chronically forgetful. And if it neither ascends nor descends, but gathers in the middle of the body in the region of the heart, then he becomes ill."

Duke Huan said, "But do ghosts really exist?"

"Indeed they do. There is the Li on the hearth5 and the Ji in the stove. The heap of clutter and trash just inside the gate is where the Leiting lives. In the northeast corner the Beia and Guilong leap about, and the northwest corner is where the Yiyang lives. In the water is the Gangxiang; on the hills, the Xin; in the mountains, the Kui;6 in the meadows, the Panghuang; and in the marshes, the Weituo."

The duke said, "May I ask what a Weituo looks like?"

Huangzi said, "The Weituo is as big as a wheel hub, as tall as a carriage shaft, has a purple robe and a vermilion hat and, as creatures go, is very ugly. When it hears the sound of thunder or a carriage, it grabs its head and stands up. Anyone who sees it will soon become a dictator.~~

Duke Huan's face lit up and he said with a laugh, "That must have been what I saw!" Then he straightened his robe and hat and sat up on the mat with Huangzi, and before the day was over, though he didn't notice it, his illness went away.

Chapter Eight:

The Liberating Principle

Philosophical Taoism, before it became overlaid by the magical and religious aspects, was very clear on the principle of *wu wei*, non-action or emptiness. In some ways *wu wei* simply means being sensitive to everything that is occurring and flowing with it. When this sensitivity is cultivated the individual becomes aware of the constraints, requirements and outcomes of the various situations in which he finds himself, and thus, in doing so, is able to tailor his activity accordingly and to decide what may be appropriate action – if any. He is able to be reflective rather than proactive and to act 'like water' in the process.

The wilfulness and waywardness of man tends to check the cosmic order of things so the solution to any problem is to stop trying to control events. If the will is resigned to the Tao – the greater scheme of things – the individual becomes an instrument of its eternal Way. This does not mean becoming passive and fatalistic but actually means becoming more involved in the wider issues of the physical plane.

The ideal person (or Perfected Man) operating in *wu wei* can act in three different ways; sometimes in only one but more often in all three. These are:

1. Effortlessness

2. Responsiveness

3. Unobtrusiveness

Chapter Eight

We have already written elsewhere of the *Chen-jen*, the true (pure) human being, the ideal figure of both philosophical and religious Taoism. The idea was first put forward by Chuang Tse and refers to people who have realized the truth within themselves and attained the Tao.

The true man is free of all limitations, has abandoned all concepts and attained total freedom. The ability to see various possibilities in situations is an aspect of wu wei, although this does mean that we must be especially alert in order to ensure that we are truly following the way that is for the Greater Good. Instead of insisting that things must be done according to his own perceptions, Perfect Man has to be aware that being obstinate will get him nowhere. He needs to understand that without making very much physical effort he can respond from his true emotional being and can unobtrusively find the point at which he fits into the wider scheme of things.

Chuang Tse uses the term *wu wei* to represent a kind of aimless wandering. This is the kind of travelling that is understood in the West as the journeying that the true hermit undertakes – being in the right place at the right time for the right reasons. Because above anything else he is in tune with himself, the sage – or wise man – does this easily. His wandering is carefree in that he is non-attached, least of all to his wandering. Earlier in the book we mentioned Chuang Tse's dream of being a butterfly. The freedom of spirit inherent in this dream is an essential quality of *wu wei*.

This quality implies that individuals are free to do as they please under any circumstances whatsoever, yet this is not quite what is meant. Their responsiveness to the input from the situations around them dictates that they find the best fit (*shi*) for themselves. Just as water finds its own level and sometimes rests as a pool – at other times becoming a waterfall – so *Chen-jen* people take care, most of the time, to remain inconspicuous and perfectly well-adjusted. When they are required to take action they do so from a point of balance. This means that they do not function from the ego or from a position of self-importance but by virtue of their perfect integration into their surroundings, like chameleons.

Wu wei is probably the Taoist principle that is the most difficult to understand. Part of this difficulty is that, for the majority of people in the West, it goes completely against the accepted mode of existence. The principle of having to put in a great deal of effort to have something take place is so entrenched in the Western psyche that to allow things to unfold in their own way, in their own time, feels like some kind of betrayal. The fact that acting at the appropriate time with the appropriate amount of force is more likely to bring about success appears to be going against the natural tide of events. We might use a quotation from *The Tao of Pooh* by Benjamin Hoff to demonstrate this:

> When you work with Wu Wei, you have no real accidents.
> Things may get a little Odd at times, but they work out.
> You don't have to try very hard to *make* them work out;
> you just *let* them.

When we learn to put ourselves in the flow of the world around us we need only expend the energy that is required for that particular moment, not energy to deal with the past or to cope with the future. Living fully in the moment means being aware, at a very subtle level, of what is going on around us. There is no point in holding on to anything for everything is transient; there is no need to do anything in particular except to sense our own energy. To get an idea of what this feels like, try the following exercise:

1. Visualize yourself standing in a fairly fast flowing river with the water coming up to your knees. The water is cool but not freezing.

2. Gradually, you become aware of the resistance you create for the water as it flows around you and you sense your skin temperature begin to drop until it is the same as that of the water.

3. You watch the water as it flows around you and you realize that it will not stop, but it will continue to accommodate you no matter what happens.

4. Begin to walk deeper into the water, becoming more and more aware as you do so of the flow of the current around you.

5. As you begin to sink beneath the water, feel yourself responding to the current, not resisting it but beginning to move with it.

6. At any point now you can allow yourself to return to reality and simply savour the feelings you have just experienced.

7. If you wish, take the exercise a little further and try to sense the effect that going with the flow has on every part of you. Note how relaxed you feel, how everything falls into place, how you seem to be revitalized by the water.

8. Finally, if you are an experienced meditator you may be able to 'dissolve' yourself in the water and become the current itself.

Always take time after an exercise such as this one to sit quietly, to become aware of your surroundings and to anchor yourself by resting your hands lightly on the ground until you feel comfortable.

Because this is an exercise, you are actually doing something, so this experience is not true *wu wei*. That is something which is as individual as you are. No-one can teach you how to experience it – you just do. As with Tao, which loses something when we use words to describe it, as we have seen, so does *wu wei*. *Wu wei*, or Emptiness, is not passivity, it is simply accepting the inevitability of what goes on around us. It is the Taoist way of life, a spontaneous form of both conscious and unconscious adeptness along the lines of least resistance.

It cannot be striven for or cultivated, and it is not time-specific. It means that we recognize that we have no need to force things to happen. We can look at everything in a fresh light and, in awaiting the fullness of events, can be much more compassionate to our fellow man, for we know that when things evolve in this way there is a rightness about them. If we have no objective or purpose within a situation, there are no expectations or goals and therefore no purpose to fulfil. We no longer strive to succeed, but can quietly accept that we are simply present in the moment.

The rambling, meandering effortless activity of the wise man as a result of this acceptance might also be called adjustment, for it is not mindless but mindful. It is never a case of 'What shall I do?' but rather a case of 'What shall I not do?' With that decision comes economy of effort, for though we might appear to be giving ourselves *carte blanche* to be lazy, in fact we are narrowing our choices to where we can take the best action. It is more often a matter of bringing influence to bear on the situation than using aggression: if we work with Tao we know that sudden force does not work but slow steady effort often does. If we can preserve emptiness within a situation we are able to focus on it to the exclusion of other diversions. This actually demonstrates a profound sense of compassion for the self, without being selfish in any way, for as soon as there is emptiness there is balance and as soon as there is balance there is the potential for peace.

Also there is a freedom from care, and again we might use the image of water to demonstrate this. As we saw with the previous exercise, water always finds its own level. In addition, depending on the force with which it is moving, it flows into any nook and cranny which may be there, taking the shape of whatever is containing it. Only when water is forceful enough will it mould its receptacle in any way – flowing round an obstacle rather than through it. Where the river bed is dry, water will dampen it, where it is wet, water will flow on. Whether it is wind-whipped or still, water retains its essential quality of being water. This then is *wu wei*.

However this presupposes that the individual responds only to external forces. In fact, in order to experience true emptiness it is more correct to think of *wu wei* as the space in which things can happen. No action need be taken and we can rest quietly awaiting events. On a personal level this means that we are open to any experience, any happening, any adjustment that occurs from within ourselves. When we are with other people, if we are 'empty space' we are non-judgemental, supportive and creative – we give people room to be themselves. In a still wider sense, the emptiness that we are is capable of perceiving the need for change, responds rather than reacts, and returns to its original state of equilibrium as rapidly as possible.

In Chinese art, space and placement are as important as the image that is painted. In *Feng Shui* we are taught the effective use of empty space; in meditation and martial arts we strive for an empty mind. In all these things the individual becomes aware of aspects of space. Even in music it is the space between the notes that comes to have as much meaning as the sound itself. The same principle of emptiness or space can be applied to any circumstances or situations around us. If we can find the *wu wei* or emptiness within a situation we are able to perceive the meaning.

By exploring and accepting such concepts, the adept is enabled to become the 'empty vessel' that we see in Taoist scriptures and is not forced into any particular set of actions, having no expectation of a particular end result. This kind of flexibility transcends the ordinary 'Live and let live' philosophy and becomes something much greater – a kind of metaphysical awareness that 'All is well.' It requires a willingness to shift contexts and see things from all sorts of different perspectives, always finding new possibilities. It is what is known in the West as lateral thinking, but the concept is taken to its highest degree.

Practice not-doing
and everything will fall into place.

Fill your bowl to the brim
and it will spill.
Keep sharpening your knife
and it will blunt.
Chase after money and security
and your heart will never unclench.
Care about people's approval
and you will be their prisoner.

Do your work, then step back.
The only path to serenity.

A further step beyond the empty vessel and the concept of non-action is no-thingness. At various points in the book we have used that particular way of writing 'nothing' quite deliberately in order to remove the idea of there being an object – a thing which is definable. An empty vessel is defined by its own edges, but no-thingness means that those edges are removed, and there is only Void.

Where there is an edge, there is light and shadow. If we return to the original meaning of *yin yang* we find this same concept in the sunny and shaded sides of the mountain. This duality is highlighted by Lao Tse where he uses contradiction to demonstrate that to experience something we must give ourselves permission to be the opposite.

If you want to become whole,
let yourself be partial.
If you want to become strait,
let yourself be crooked.
If you want to become full,
let yourself be empty.
If you want to be reborn,
let yourself die . . .

When we lose our boundaries and go beyond these contrasts, that which is external to us is the same as we are. In this way we reach Unity and the concept of Oneness. This understanding of Oneness leads us to the appreciation of life's events and our place within them as simple miraculous moments which 'just are'. This involves being completely absorbed in whatever you are doing or being, with your full attention and abilities called into play in the here and now so that there is no division between you yourself and what you are doing. The energy that you are focusing on the task in hand is you and you and the task are inseparable. This is one of the reasons why *ching* or life essence is so important to followers of the Tao and why it is so important to replenish *chi*.

The energy that is expended in Emptiness is phenomenal, but in the long run is not exhausting, or exhausted, for this is as it should be and if we are in Tao we have as much as we need at our disposal. If we allow the power to flow through us like water then we are fulfilling our life-task. This concept ultimately brings us to the realization that even the death of the physical body can have no true power. Lao Tse says:

> Though you lose the body, you do not die.

Or, put another way,

> To die but not to perish is to be eternally present.

Chuang Tse has a similar perspective when he talks of the ancients of his own time who clearly had had an awareness and acceptance of the cycle of life and death that we in the modern world sometimes have difficulty in reaching. He does not discount an emotional response when he talks of their joys and their sorrows, but the implication is that in not 'supplementing the natural by human means' they practise *wu wei*. He writes:

> The true men of old did not know what it was to love life or to hate death. They did not rejoice in birth, nor strive to put off dissolution. Unconcerned they came and unconcerned they went. That was all. They did not forget whence it was they had sprung, neither did they seek to inquire their return thither. Cheerfully they accepted life, waiting patiently for their restoration (the end). This is what is called not to lead the heart astray from Tao, and not to supplement the natural by human means. Such a one may be called a true man. Such men are free in mind and calm in demeanour, with

high foreheads. Sometimes disconsolate like autumn, and sometimes warm like spring, their joys and sorrows are in direct touch with the four seasons, in harmony with all creation and none know the limit thereof.

Chuang Tse also writes very tellingly of what the Taoist attitude to death is. It encompasses the idea of rebirth but also gives clear information of the acceptance of death and continuation in one form or another. The story below suggests that however philosophical one might be about life and death, it is the individual's handling of himself and his attitudes that ultimately gives him ease and comfort.

Four men, Tsesze, Tseyu, Tseli, and Tselai, were conversing together, saying, 'Whoever can make Not-being the head, Life the backbone, and Death the tail, and whoever realizes that death and life and being and non-being are of one body, that man shall be admitted to friendship with us.' The four looked at each other and smiled, and completely understanding one another, became friends accordingly. By-and-by, Tseyu fell ill, and Tsesze went to see him. 'Verily the Creator is great!' said the sick man. 'See how He has doubled me up.' His back was so hunched that his viscera were at the top of his body. His cheeks were level with his navel, and his shoulders were higher than his neck. His neck bone pointed up towards the sky. The whole economy of his organism was deranged, but his mind was calm as ever. He dragged himself to a well, and said, 'Alas, that God should have doubled me up like this!'

'Do you dislike it?' asked Tsesze. 'No, why should I?' replied Tseyu. 'If my left arm should become a cock, I should be able to herald the dawn with it. If my right arm should become a sling, I should be able to shoot down a bird to broil with it. If my buttocks should become wheels, and my spirit become a horse, I should be able to ride in it

Chapter Eight

– what need would I have of a chariot? I obtained life because it was my time, and I am now parting with it in accordance with Tao. Content with the coming of things in their time and living in accord with Tao, joy and sorrow touch me not. This is, according to the ancients, to be freed from bondage. Those who cannot be freed from bondage are so because they are bound by the trammels of material existence. But man has ever given way before God; why, then, should I dislike it?'

By-and-by, Tselai fell ill, and lay gasping for breath, while his family stood weeping around. Tseli went to see him, and cried to the wife and children: 'Go away! You are impeding his dissolution.' Then, leaning against the door, he said, 'Verily, God is great! I wonder what He will make of you now, and whither He will send you. Do you think he will make you into a rat's liver or into an insect leg?'

'A son,' answered Tselai, 'must go whithersoever his parents bid him, East, West, North, or South. Yin and Yang are no other than a man's parents. If Yin and Yang bid me die quickly, and I demur, then the fault is mine, not theirs. The Great (universe) gives me this form, this toil in manhood, this repose in old age, this rest in death. Surely that which is such a kind arbiter of my life is the best arbiter of my death.'

'Suppose that the boiling metal in a smelting-pot were to bubble up and say, "Make of me a Moyeh!" I think the master caster would reject that metal as uncanny. And if simply because I am cast into a human form, I were to say, "Only a man! only a man!" I think the Creator too would reject me as uncanny. If I regard the universe as the smelting pot, and the Creator as the Master Caster, how should I worry wherever I am sent?' Then he sank into a peaceful sleep and waked up very much alive.

Chuang Tse also muses in his own inimitable way about the state of being dead and supposes that death will, in fact, change the soul's perspective. The life we live may not after all be the true reality. He asks:

> How do I know that enjoying life is not a delusion? How do I know that in hating death we are not like people who got lost in early childhood and do not know the way home? Lady Li was the child of a border guard in Ai. When first captured by the state of Jin, she wept so much her clothes were soaked. But after she entered the palace, shared the king's bed, and dined on the finest meats, she regretted her tears. How do I know that the dead do not regret their previous longing for life?

In the simple tale of his mourning for his wife, he shows a fine appreciation of the meaning of existence before life, a return to Oneness and a celebration of the change of state which is death. In 'this confused amorphous realm' we have emptiness, then 'something changed' and his wife's life began. Now her life was returning to its source and he should celebrate rather than mourn.

> When Chuang Tse's wife died and Hui Shi came to convey his condolences, he found Chuang Tse squatting with his knees out, drumming on a pan and singing. 'You lived with her, she raised your children, and you grew old together,' Hui Shi said. 'Not weeping when she died would have been bad enough. Aren't you going too far by drumming on a pan and singing?'

> 'No,' Chuang Tse said, 'when she first died how could I have escaped feeling the loss? Then I looked back to the beginning before she had life. Not only before she had life but before she had form. Not only before she had form, but before she had vital energy. In this confused amorphous realm, something changed and vital energy appeared – when the vital energy was changed, form

appeared; with changes in form, life began. Now there is another change bringing death. This is like the progression of the four seasons of spring and autumn, winter and summer. Here she was lying down to sleep in a huge room and I followed her sobbing and wailing. When I realized my actions showed I hadn't understood destiny, I stopped.'

This truly is *wu wei* in all its magnificence. It is non-action within action, emptiness and no-thingness all rolled into one.

THOUGHTS AND IDEAS

At this point we explore the art of doing nothing, a concept which is foreign to the Western mind. Emptiness inevitably leaves space for other things to happen, and if we can we must get to the point where we can let things be. These quotes reflect this, and allow us to contemplate 'not-being' that is the natural process of death.

'To live outside the law you must be honest...'
Bob Dylan

The noblest joy of the senses, the holiest peace of the heart, the most resplendent lustre of all good works derives from this: That the creature put his or her heart wholly into what he or she does.
Mechtild of Magdeburg

Inaction
The follower of knowledge learns as much as he can every day;
The follower of the Way forgets as much as he can every day.
By attrition he reaches a state of inaction
Wherein he does nothing, but nothing remains undone.
To conquer the world, accomplish nothing;
If you must accomplish something,
The world remains beyond conquest.
Charles Muller

Decay and Renewal
Empty the self completely;
Embrace perfect peace.
The world will rise and move;
Watch it return to rest.
All the flourishing things
Will return to their source.
This return is peaceful;
It is the flow of nature,
An eternal decay and renewal.
Accepting this brings enlightenment,
Ignoring this brings misery

Taking No Action
The external world is fragile,
and he who meddles with its natural way,
risks causing damage to himself.
He who tries to grasp it,
thereby loses it.
It is natural for things to change,
sometimes being ahead, sometimes behind.
There are times when even breathing
may be difficult,
whereas its natural state is easy.
Sometimes one is strong,
and sometimes weak,
sometimes healthy,
and sometimes sick,
sometimes is first,
and at other times behind.
The sage does not try
to change the world by force,
for he knows that force results in force.
He avoids extremes and excesses,
and does not become complacent.
Stan Rosenthal

To the sage, neither death nor life makes any change in him,
and how much less should the consideration of advantage
and injury do so!

Plato was discoursing on his theory of ideas and, pointing to the
cups on the table before him, said while there are many cups in
the world, there is only one 'idea' of a cup, and this cupness
precedes the existence of all particular cups.
"I can see the cup on the table," interrupted Diogenes,
"but I can't see the 'cupness'".
"That's because you have the eyes to see the cup," said Plato,
"but", tapping his head with his forefinger, "you don't have the
intellect with which to comprehend 'cupness'."
Diogenes walked up to the table, examined a cup and, looking
inside, asked, "Is it empty?"
Plato nodded.
"Where is the 'emptiness' which precedes this empty cup?"
asked Diogenes.
Plato allowed himself a few moments to collect his thoughts, but
Diogenes reached over and, tapping Plato's head with his finger,
said "I think you will find here is the 'emptiness'."

The mind from the beginning is of pure nature, but since there is
the finite aspect of it which is sullied by finite views, there is the
sullied aspect of it. Although there is this defilement, yet the
original pure nature is eternally unchanged. This mystery the
Enlightened One alone understands.'
Tibetan Book of the Dead

When Zhuangzi went to Chu, he saw an old skull, all dry and parched. He poked it with his carriage whip and then asked, "Sir, were you greedy for life and forgetful of reason, and so came to this? Was your state overthrown and did you bow be-neath the axe and so came to this? Did you do some evil deed and were you ashamed to bring disgrace upon your parents and fam-ily, and so came to this? Was it through the pangs of cold and hunger that you came to this? Or did your springs and autumns pile up until they brought you to this?"

When he had finished speaking, he dragged the skull over and, using it for a pillow, lay down to sleep.

In the middle of the night, the skull came to him in a dream and said, "You chatter like a rhetorician and all your words betray the entanglements of a living man.

The dead know nothing of these! Would you like to hear a lecture on the dead?" "Indeed," said Zhuangzi.

The skull said, "Among the dead there are no rulers above, no subjects below, and no chores of the four seasons. With nothing to do, our springs and autumns are as endless as heaven and earth. A king facing south on his throne could have no more happiness than this!"

Zhuangzi couldn't believe this and said "If I got the Arbiter of Fate to give you a body again, make you some flesh, return you to your parents and family and your and friends, you would want that, wouldn't you?"

The skull frowned severely, wrinkling up its brow "Why would I throw away more happiness than that of a throne and take on the troubles of a human being again?

But to wear out your brain trying to make things into one without
realizing that they are all the same-this is called "three in the
morning." What do I mean by "three in the morning"? When the
monkey trainer was handing out acorns, he said, "You get three in
the morning and four at night." This made all the monkeys
furious. "Well, then," he said, "you get four in the morning and
three at night." The monkeys were all delighted.
There was no change in the reality behind the words, and yet the
monkeys responded with joy and anger. Let them, if they want to.
So the sage harmonizes with both right and wrong and rests in
Heaven the Equalizer. This is called walking two roads.

The Invocator of the Ancestors, dressed in his black, square-cut
robes, peered into the pigpen and said, "Why should you object
to dying? I'm going to fatten you for three months, practice aus-
terities for ten days, fast for three days, spread the white rushes,
and lay your shoulders and rump on the carved sacrificial stand –
you'll go along with that, won't you? True, if I were planning
things from the point of view of a pig, I'd say is would be better
to eat chaff and bran and stay right there in the pen. But if I were
planning for myself, I'd say that if I could be hon-oured as a high
official while I lived, and get to ride in a fine hearse and lie among
the feathers and trappings when I died, I'd go along with that.
Speaking for the pig, I'd give such a life a flat refusal, but speaking
for myself, I'd certainly accept. I wonder why I look at things
differently from a pig?"

Chapter Nine:

Meditation and Practice of Tao

When discussing *Chi Gung*, we mentioned the flow of *chi* (energy) within the body. Taoists believe that there is an even more subtle energy which is produced in order to maintain life as a physical entity. This is the life-essence, or life-force, known as ching that we first mentioned in Chapter One. It might be called primordial energy and it is a vital and integral part of Taoist thought.

Ching develops in the body close to the 'lower cinnabar field' that we have already met as the *tan tien* (point of power). First to form in a baby after conception is the *ching* – the germ of life, seed essence or essence of bodily organs. It is only then that the brain and spinal cord begin to form. It is believed that the entity has been given a finite amount of energy available to it for use in physical life. In ancient works on the subject, *ching* and *chi* unite to transmit the characteristics of the parents to the child.

Taoist adepts do their best to conserve *ching*, recognizing that when the body is depleted by illness, this basic energy can be used up: when it totally exhausted it results in the death of the physical entity. This conservation of energy can take place either through various sexual practices – akin to Tantric yoga – or through meditation and other 'exercises of the mind'. This is why present-day doctors now believe that the more mentally aware elderly people remain, the better chance there is of good health.

One of the basic beliefs of the Taoist practitioner is that *chi* responds to intention. This means that it can be directed to any part of the body. When the mind is confused, it becomes extremely difficult to focus intention. When this happens, the *chi* becomes much weaker and more feeble. *Chi* must be strengthened and renewed to the point where intention can be regenerated and the mind becomes tranquil. This is done by consciously allowing the energy to sink down to the lower *tan tien* (point of power in the abdomen) where it can be worked with. The theory behind this is that the mind, intention and energy all need to be in a state of balance, supporting one another.

The most efficient way to achieve this is through the practice of meditation. While many Buddhist practices have transferred easily to Taoist belief and been enhanced or changed in the process, some meditation practices show their common source. Anyone with a knowledge of other meditation practices will see many similarities. Setting aside about 30 minutes a day for meditation is at least calming and at best strengthens *chi* and therefore conserves *ching*. Meditation might also be thought of as 'mindfulness' – that is, retaining an awareness of what one is doing – so all actions and movements (either standing or sitting) can be considered to be practising meditation. *Chi Gung* and *Tai Chi Chuan* and, of course, internal alchemy all lead one towards inner contemplation and ultimately the practice of meditation.

Wear comfortable, loose clothing, ensure you are warm enough and that your breathing is unrestricted and even. It is worthwhile taking a few moments to practise a few stretching or *Chi Gung* exercises to focus the mind. Preferably set aside the same time each day and make sure you will not be disturbed – this is an important part of your own self-discipline. Avoid meditating within an hour of eating. In order to pique your interest, a few simple meditations are described below.

Wu Chi Standing

Begin the meditation by taking up the *Wu Chi* (Emptiness) stance. This is one of the rudimentary postures for both *Tai Chi* and *Chi Gung* practice.

1. Keep your body erect but not stiffly upright.

2. Stand with your legs a shoulder-width apart and slightly bent at the knee, with your feet parallel.

3. Your breathing should be steady and even, breathing out for a little longer than you breath in. Beginners will find the rhythm of four/six easy to manage.

Standing Pole Tan Tien Focus

1. When you are comfortable in the above stance, become aware as you breathe in through your nose of your *tan tien* and the expansion of your abdomen.

2. As you breathe out – either through your nose or mouth – be aware of the abdomen contracting.

3. Focus your mind on the area of the lower *tan tien* where the *Chihai* or 'Sea of Chi' is situated.

4. As you breathe in, imagine fresh *Chi* from the universe entering your body and flowing into the *Chihai* (the reservoir of power).

5. As you breath out, imagine the used up energy leaving your body and returning to Source where it will be renewed.

If you can, continue to do this for about ten minutes and feel the power of the *chi* as you store it in your body. Do not worry if you experience tingling, sensations of heat or other unusual feelings; this is simply your energy realigning itself. When you feel your meditation is complete, simply allow your focus to shift to an awareness of your whole body and then to your surroundings. Don't try to force this exercise, and spend as little or as much time as you can although you may find that you can continue for a considerable length of time as you become more proficient.

Chi Flow Meditation

In the meditation above you learned how to focus your *chi*. This meditation is a simple one which enables you to experience the sensation of *chi* flow through your body. Here you learn how to bring your *chi* under the control of your intention – that is, to deliberately circulate it throughout your body. A more advanced form is the meditation on the Microcosmic Cycle seen later in this chapter.

The easiest way to initially accomplish the circulation of *chi* is to adopt the same stance with the 'beachball' as you did with the first part of the 'Draw a Bow to Shoot an Arrow' exercise in the *Chi Gung* section in Chapter Six. With regular practice you should be able to hold this stance for some time. Your breathing should be slow and rhythmic.

After a short period you will become conscious of sensations in your body – especially in your arms and the palms of your hands. Without focusing on any one area in particular, just observe these sensations for a few moments.

When ready, focus your mind on an area in which you are especially aware of *chi* activity. As with the Standing Pole *Tan Tien* Focus meditation it might feel warm, cold, tingly, itchy and so on. There are no right or wrong sensations – simply be aware of what you are experiencing. Initially, it may seem as though nothing is happening, but by increasingly focusing your awareness you are bringing your intention to bear on the flow of *chi*.

Now direct that energy to flow smoothly throughout the body, nourishing and enhancing the function of every part of it. You may find that you become aware of separate sensations as if the energy were travelling along separate lines. This is an awareness of the meridians (lines of power) within the body.

Adopt your own rhythm of breathing, directing the *chi* with the in-breath and moving it forward with the exhalation. If it is easier for you to do so, as you exhale visualize the new chi flowing into the space left by the old. Remember that by focusing and renewing your own *chi* you are also making a very subtle but strong link with the Tao (Universal Energy).

The Five Elements Colour Meditation

For this meditation, which is designed to cleanse and energize the five major *yin* (or *zang*) organs of the body and, by association, their five corresponding *yang* (*fu*) organs, you may need to remind yourself of the Five Phases system. This is the system mentioned earlier in the book whereby the Five Elements support, or are supported by, one another.

1. Adopt a sitting position – either upright on the edge of a straight seat or cross-legged on the floor. If you find this latter position uncomfortable, use a cushion to support your buttocks so that you feel you have a firm connection with the ground. This cross-legged posture is a classic meditation one. When you feel settled and ready, hold your hands in your lap facing upwards, with the back of the right hand resting lightly in the palm of the left.

2. Begin by allowing your mind to focus on the lower tan tien area. If it helps, use your extended thumbs and fingers to circle the area. Co-ordinate your inhalation and exhalation until you feel calm and centred. As white light is often easier for the beginner to work with, begin the meditation by focusing first on the Lungs and its meridian as per the table below. You can of course begin with any organ provided you maintain the correct correspondences.

3. Lungs are deemed to be ruled by the Metal element, so visualize an intense white light entering the Lungs each time you inhale. This light is used to cleanse every part of the Lung system. Because the Large Intestine is paired in the zang-fu system with the Lungs, the energy you generate will have an effect on this system as well.

4. As you perceive the white light flooding into your lungs as you breathe in, as you breathe out, see yourself letting go of the murky, dim light that represents your blocked energy and resultant unhappiness. You may find that at this point Grief, which you did not know you were still holding, rises to the surface. Simply allow it to do so, note it and continue the meditation until such time as that you feel any difficulties, either physical or emotional, have been helped.

5. Having taken note of the table below and when you feel ready, use the colours to work with the four other zang-fu systems. Remembering that each colour is associated with an Element, focus strongly on the colour of your choice. As you breathe out visualize the dull, stale colour taking all your negativity and the negative aspects of the associated emotion with it. Bear in mind the way that the Elements interact with one another. It is unwise to follow one Element with another which conflicts directly with it – for example, you would be advised not to follow Fire with Water as the one would cancel out the other's benefits.

6. When you have worked with all five systems, return your attention to your lower tan tien. Perceive all five colours – often seen as a stream of iridescent mother-of-pearl light – flowing through your body. Allow this light to flow from the top of your head, down through your spine to your coccyx. You might then experience the energy as warmth in that area.

7. Gradually become aware of your surroundings once more and orientate yourself by touching the ground with your fingertips. Become aware of your connection with the earth and with nature in general.

Colour	Zang Organ	Associated Fu Organ	Emotion
White	Lungs	Large Intestine	Grief
Red	Heart	Small Intestine	Joy
Yellow	Spleen	Stomach	Pensiveness
Blue/Green	Liver	Gall Bladder	Anger
Deep Blue/Black	Kidneys	Bladder	Fear

As always, this meditation is designed to make a firm connection between the breath (*chi*), the mind and the intention. Below are some simple ways of learning to control your mind.

1. *Stop and observe*. Here you learn how thoughts arise and wither away in the mind, particularly if they are not encouraged. You are practising the beginnings of the art of *wu wei* (Emptiness), learning how to simply allow thoughts to come and go, without necessarily holding onto them. When you are not attached to any particular emotion, you are able to hold back and simply note the passage of a thought, an idea or a concept. This allows you to ignore rambling thoughts so that they do not intrude on the focus of your mind at any one point. Not only does this help in meditation, it also allows you, with training, to concentrate on any task in hand without having to pay attention to the clamour and clatter of the everyday world.

2. *Observe and imagine*. This allows you to create an image or symbol on which you can concentrate. Such a method focuses the mind and shifts your attention away from the 'chatterbox' which is your mind as it functions in the everyday world. As you begin to travel the Taoist path you are enabled to use symbols, ideas and concepts which initially may be foreign to you, but actually resound on a very deep level. When working with *chi*, or any other concept of energy, it is helpful to be able to visualize the energy centres as spheres of vibrant light.

3. Using intention. *Ching* (essence), *chi* (energy) and *shen* (power or spirit) are the fundamental concepts of meditative breathing, often called the 'Three Treasures'. When you have learned to keep your emotional mind calm and your breath controlled, you are ready to learn to focus attention on your internal energy. Learning how to use these Three Treasures, enhancing them and guiding them through the meridian network, is an integral part of working with the Tao. We have already begun this process in the meditations above and can begin now to raise energy from the sacrum to the head to nourish the spirit and brain. To do this, we focus on the *Chihai* then move energy from there down to the perineum, up through the coccyx, and up along the subtle spiritual centres along the spine and up into the head. This is the first part of what is known as the Microcosmic Orbit.

The human body is a 'little world' and the Microcosmic Orbit is the circulation of *yin-yang* energy within the body, which is thought to mirror the way that energy circulates in nature (from positive to negative and back again). Opening the Microcosmic Orbit is one of the first and most important Taoist meditations. Using the breath (*chi*), energy is increased at each major spiritual centre or acupuncture point along each of the primary *yin-yang* meridians.

The line of power known as the Governor Channel (*yang*) runs up the spine to the inside of the skull. It meets the Functional Channel (*yin*) in the mouth, at the upper palate. This channel runs down the front of the body to the perineum, where it again becomes the Governor channel. This is why in many exercises the tongue is placed against the roof of the mouth to act as a bridge between the two channels and was mentioned in the earlier information on *Chi Gung* in Chapter Seven. The relatively simple meditation to open the Microcosmic Orbit ultimately feeds energy into all the meridian systems of the body. The illustration opposite demonstrates the circulation of the energy.

Microcosmic Orbit Circulation

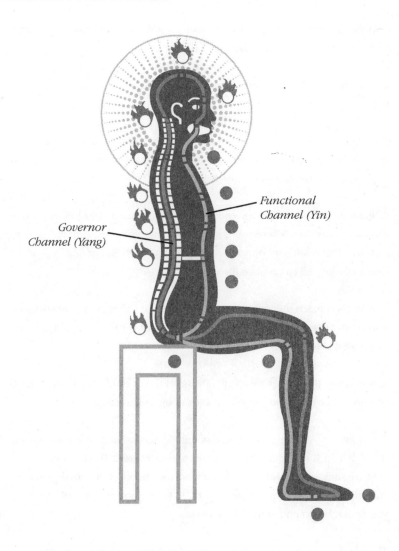

Functional
Channel (Yin)

Governor
Channel (Yang)

Chapter Nine

Microcosmic Orbit

1. Begin as you did with the Five Elements Colour Meditation and centre yourself in your lower *tan tien*.

2. Sense a sphere of white light in your *Chihai* and allow it to sink gently down to your perineum.

3. Gently move the sphere up your spine, in accordance with the above diagram, stopping at each centre as illustrated. Check at each point that you are happy with the quality of the light.

4. Reinforce the power and the energy of the light at each point before moving on to the next one. Where you have noticed discrepancies, you may wish to return to that point later on to discover what the blockages might be. For the moment continue to circulate the energy.

5. When you reach the last point on the Governor Channel, ensure that your tongue is placed gently behind your teeth to effect the bridge as already mentioned above.

6. Now allow the energy to sink gently down the front of your body towards your lower *tan tien* again, pausing at each point as illustrated.

7. Continue to circulate the sphere of light in this fashion, gradually sensing that the light is becoming more and more internalized. Three circuits of the light are sufficient to rejuvenate and refresh the energy of the physical, mental and spiritual bodies but you may continue for as long as you wish provided you remember to end in the lower *tan tien*.

The physical benefits of the Microcosmic Orbit are an increased resistance to physical disease, emotional problems and spiritual difficulties. You have made available to yourself much more of the energy of the Tao and will therefore benefit from an understanding of, and empathy with, all those myriad aspects of Nature which belong to The Way.

The sense of balance in all aspects of life are an integral part of your journey along the path which eventually takes you to an understanding of *wu-wei* and the real meaning of emptiness. Free from all attachments, poised within your own universe, you welcome Life and all its vicissitudes and glories and are ready to enjoy the benefits of a long and happy existence. When you have become proficient at performing the Microcosmic Orbit, you will find that many of the more obscure meanings of the Taoist Scriptures become apparent to you.

Over the centuries, the various systems of exercise and self-development – touched on only briefly in the preceding chapters – have led to many different ways of exploring the Tao. We have chosen the simplest, to give a taster of the myriad ways which are available to you.

One of the ways in which Taoists regard health and spiritual knowledge is in the theory of the Theory of the Nine Palaces which is seen in some Taoist texts. This states that the brain is divided into nine compartments which are inhabited by different deities. The seat of the highest body deity (*Tai-i*) is at the centre of the head and is called *ni-huan* similar to Nirvana in Buddhism while the other palaces are arranged in two rows between the forehead and the nape of the neck. The most important ones are the first three 'palaces' of the lower row where *Huang-lao-chun* and his assistants reside.

Other texts suggest that these palaces rule the bodily organs – the heart, kidneys, liver, lungs, pancreas, gall bladder, small intestine, large intestine and bladder. It is an easy step in the light of modern medical knowledge to suspect that the texts were referring to aspects of the endocrine system which have always played such an important part in health and well-being. Taoists believe that there will always be communication with the deities and that part of ourselves which has the potential to be immortal.

Taoism is a polytheistic religion, which means that it has a number of deities. Its divinities form a pantheon of Immortals divided into three levels.

The first level is comprised of the Lordly Spirits of Anterior Heaven which have existed since before Heaven and Earth divided. They include the Three Pristine Ones (the highest divinities); the Four Heavenly Ministers (four deities in charge of all things in Heaven and Earth); the Stellar Sovereigns of the Five Planets and Seven Stars (Taoism worships the Seven Stars as spirits and calls them Stellar Sovereigns); the Four Numinous Animals (the Blue Dragon, the White Tiger, the Red Phoenix and the Black Warrior control the four directions); and the Twenty-Eight Constellations (the signs of the fixed star areas which the sun and moon pass by according to the ancient astronomers).

The second level is comprised of Perfect Immortals who have attained Tao after the creation of Heaven and Earth. That is, they were ordinary mortals who, through study and good deeds (cultivating Tao), became Immortals. They were called the Divinities of Posterior Heaven. The Eight Immortals belong to this level as does the Motherly Matriarch who protects seafarers.

The third level is made up of the lesser divinities of popular religion who are recognized by Taoism. This is because of the original belief that everything contained spirit. Later belief meant that many of these spirits had to be placated as much as honoured.

By the time that a practitioner has reached such a level of understanding he is ready to move forward on the next stage of his Tao.

Discipleship

Because Early Taoism was an oral tradition where knowledge was passed down individually from master to student, the act of formally becoming a disciple to a famous master was really the only way to learn and to further one's studies.

This formal acceptance not only established the relationship with the master, it was also the first step in entering the Tao, since the master was then able to assess the pupil's suitability for the tasks ahead: temperamentally not everyone was suited to the rigorous disciplines. Initially, it was not even considered that one could become a master until one had been practising for many years, so the commitment to study was an important one.

Today this method of transmission may still be followed – beginners first follow their masters to learn the scriptures and commandments. During this period, masters can teach some knowledge and techniques, as well as observe the disciple's behaviour. If his character is suitable, he can be recommended to receive registration and become an initiate.

Previously it was required that the pupil renounced his family, though in today's world this is not always possible. Acts of renunciation are often seen in other spiritual disciplines; for instance, Jesus commanded his disciples to leave their fishing nets (their livelihood) and follow him. Such an act symbolizes the renunciation of the old way of life for a new one and must be done willingly. The Taoist scriptures promise that:

> As he has left his family and followed his master's instructions, he will surely become a Perfect Man.

As we have seen, the family unit has been important in Chinese culture so this action also represented setting out into the unknown and an individual adopting his own particular path or Way.

It is an especially important aspect of religious Taoism to study at the feet of a master and to search for the Immortals; when Taoists go on a tour to seek for Perfect Men and study Tao this is called 'Wandering About'. Translated literally from the Chinese, the phrase is 'to wander like a cloud'. There was no custom of Wandering About when Taoism was first established, although it does pick up on the imagery of Lao Tse packing up his worldly goods and walking over the border never to be seen again.

Many Taoists chose this special way, using ascetic practice, to harden and discipline themselves as well as to test their religious belief and will. In the time of the *Wei* and *Jin* Dynasties and later when the division between North and South occurred, Taoism continued to spread its scriptures and also to separate into different sects. Chang Yuchu, who was the 43rd Celestial Master in the Ming dynasty, declared:

> Once a Daoist, one must get rid of all the emotions of this world, and return to Perfection by giving up all desires. He must take it his duty to explore his mind and nourish his spiritual essence. He must practice the Daoist commandments, and discipline himself by bearing loneliness accompanied only by a bamboo hat and a bamboo bowl. Sometimes when coming to a cave mansion in a famous mountain, he can settle down to visit a venerable Taoist so as to study Tao, the meaning of life, the source of spiritual essence, and the essence of virtue. Thus he is perfectly aware of Tao and meditates on the chaos of the universe without taking fame or wealth into consideration. He will not change his mind in spite of hardship, he will be resolute in spite of his poverty and humble situation, and polite and modest in spite of humiliation. Thus he can purify his spiritual essence, with a strong will as well as softness and mildness in his heart.

Part of Wandering About was learning to trust the universe for what was needed and therefore Taoists needed to be provided with the ability to make a living wherever they were. It is this practice which gave rise to the Taoist arts, be they magic – as in driving out evil – calligraphy, astrology, geomancy or painting. The wanderer would use what he had learned as a disciple in the service of others.

In today's society, particularly as Taoism spreads beyond the borders of China through the dissemination of the Taoist arts of *Feng Shui*, *Tai Chi* and *Chi Gung*, the Taoist practitioner has the whole world in which to wander about and find knowledge. He is less likely to have the opportunity to devote all his time to study, but often his wandering will take him back to the roots of Taoism in the sacred mountains and temples of China.

Provided his everyday work brings him a modicum of satisfaction – this also being a requirement of Tao – he can use his leisure time to pursue his search for Tao and the cultivation of his life essence. He may still study under a master and at the same time also carry out his family responsibilities. Thus it is possible for him in many different ways to earn himself the title of *jushi* which means 'lay Taoist'.

The Buddhists first introduced the idea of the renunciation of one's family, but they also recognized that it was not always possible for everyone to do this, so the principle of being a layman while still carrying out the correct rituals was accepted from antiquity. In Taoism, how the practitioner carried out the requirements of his own beliefs would depend upon which sect he belonged to.

Morning and Evening Rites

Religious practice for Taoists incorporate morning and evening rites particularly in temples. For the lone Taoist, the term 'Rites' refers to reading a portion of Taoist scriptures aloud, both morning and evening. Obviously this can be incorporated into one's regular practice, whether that is meditation or physical exercise.

There are no ancient records in existence about Morning and Evening Rites in early Taoism, although as mentioned in *On Conducting the Pervasive Mystery Numinous Treasure Three Grottoes Rituals and Commandments for Worshipping the Tao* in the Northern and Southern dynasties, Taoists practised the 'Rites of Routine Practice'. By the time of the compilation of the Essential Books of the Taoist Canon in the Qing Dynasty, there are two scriptures about them. One is the *Pristine Subtlety Taoist Rites of the Great Discipline*, the other is the *Book of the Supreme Taoist Rites*.

The Morning Rites consist of three parts:

1. Incantations
2. Scriptures
3 . Exhortations

The Evening Rites have two parts:

1. Scriptures (e.g. The *Sublime Book of the Supreme Numinous Treasure Pervasive Mystery for Saving from Distress in the Ten Directions*).
2. Exhortations (e.g. the *Treasure Exhortation of the Big Dipper*).

The Rites will vary slightly from sect to sect and from place to place. Morning rites are normally practised from 5 a.m. to 7 a.m. since this is the time of day when the Yang *chi* or Vital Breath is rising and the Yin *chi* is inactive. At that time no food is taken and the *chi* is even. Morning rites have the effect of clearing the orifices of the body, strengthening the pulse and bringing peace of mind.

At the other end of the day, the evening rites are often conducted from 5 p.m. to 7 p.m. when the Yang breath and power is much weaker whereas the Yin breath becomes strong. The body is stale, with unhealthy toxins building up. Just as in the West an exercise session can rejuvenate the system, so carrying out the Evening Rites can renew your energy and bring about relaxation and tranquillity.

It is more than possible that morning and evening rites were adopted from the Buddhist religion, but as a daily discipline it allows the practitioner to cultivate Tao and to contemplate Immortality. Finding the right way to practise gives him the potential to refine his body and regain access to his perfect inner nature. He thus maximizes his own opportunity for health, wellbeing and spiritual knowledge.

The Taoist practitioner ultimately has access to a whole plethora of spiritual assistance. He has a choice of paths in front of him and will initially follow whichever one suits his own temperament. Philosophical Taoism and the richness of thought woven into that will satisfy one part, the energetic component of the physical disciplines will satisfy another and the rituals and connectedness of religious Taoism will create sanctuary for that part which needs nurturing. In the end he comes to realize that by nurturing chi and being aware of how he uses that precious commodity most effectively he moves beyond the boundaries of his own being and has access to Tao and its limitless power and potential.

Integrating Meditation

There comes a time when the practitioner wishes to take Taoist meditation further and try to integrate it into their lives in a more powerful way. At that point he will need to enhance his practice and learn to circulate the energy of *Chi* in all sorts of different ways. We have looked fairly extensively at the Five Elements and a little thought will make it obvious that there are distinctly different types of personalities within those Five Elements. Getting to know oneself means that we learn how the various energies work within us and what essential energies are important to us. One very important consideration when one studies Taoist meditation in depth is the discovery that there is a distinct difference between the physical body and what is called the *Chi* body. This is the more subtle body which approximates to the Aura or essential energy in Western thought.

Initially, as you become more proficient at circulating Chi, for instance in the Microcosmic Orbit, you will gradually become aware that you need to focus more fully internally on certain of the Five Elements. Individually, each person has their own unique balance of elements. For instance, a person with a predominance of the earth element would initially concentrate on sexuality and his basic life energy, the way he presents himself to the world and making the body very strong, whereas a metal person would want to focus on developing mental clarity, flexibility and making their body very supple.

As the energy becomes freer and the physical body reacts and changes to this input of meditative energy, we can turn our attention to the emotions. In the energy of the body or cellular memory there is an imprint of everything we have ever done, thought or been. In some ways we are like a computer which has been storing information since the moment we were conceived. Unfortunately, this information is not held in separate files which can just be deleted, the files are all linked together and each one has an effect on the others. When we make adjustments to one aspect of life it impinges on others.

These imprints are the conditioning of our personalities and often the energy gets trapped within the tissues of the body, giving rise to aches, pains and difficulties. When we begin to deal with these, it releases the energy and we then have to deal with the cause. Generally we should deal with the stuck negative emotions first, which might be called the lower level emotions; for example, hate, depression, anger, vindictiveness.

We saw in Chapter Six that the Fire technique for working with *Chi* is more direct and the Water technique more gradual, making it easier to dissolve difficulties. By and large with emotions it is more successful to dissolve them by going into the energy channels of the body and dealing with them bit-by-bit and piece-by-piece. The dissolving techniques are done to ensure there is a free flow of energy and that the negative stuck energy can be transformed and moved beyond the confines of the physical body. Then the Chi field has more of an effect on the people round about. Your own personal field actually has the ability to reach into the infinite.

As soon as you start clearing your own energy field you will find that you are more in control of your life and are less likely to find that energies from your external environment have an effect on you. Initially you may find that you become very sensitive to all sorts of subtle influences around from other people's emotions, but gradually you will find that your daily practice helps you to deal with the additional input.

Forces from beyond the world in which we live can also shape our environment. The Taoist sage recognizes the effect that the stars and their energy fields have on his life and uses that knowledge to help him reach his Tao. The unresolved blockages in the practitioner's being resonate in a particular way to the planetary input, which means that old patterns can come back to haunt us when we least expect it.

Regular circulation of *Chi* is essential for individual health. Healing the physical body, having an effect on the glandular system and the internal organs and then working on emotional blockages, transforms the way that you present yourself to the rest of the world and how the world approaches you. Practicing how to move energy through your channels and knowing why you are doing it allows you to have far more of a sense of purpose in life and can make you very aware of the misuse of energy. There is no longer any necessity to waste energy needlessly or to block your responses to circumstances around you.

It is for this reason that some people may find that they go through a period of celibacy. This should not be enforced but can be observed as a natural part of the process of growth towards maturity. Earlier we saw that the practitioner will tend to respond to the requirements of his or her basic element type – this is nowhere more true than in the question of sexual activity and celibacy. Those who choose to be celibate will tend to use more of the sitting meditations or other techniques like *tai chi chuan* which are the moving ones. Standing meditations tend to work on the physical body, seated meditations on the emotional being and moving meditations work on either or both.

Ultimately, of course, they are all destined to work on a more spiritual plane, leading to union with the Tao. Those who choose to share their energies will have learned to circulate their own energies first and then to reach beyond themselves towards other people, without fear of either being depleted or of depleting others.

It is quite important to sound a note of warning at this point. *Chi* energy should never be used as a weapon or a tool and least of all in the sexual sense. To use it in this way goes against every tenet of Taoist thought. *Chi* is a very powerful energy and should always be treated with great respect. This does not preclude it being used in order to help others dissolve their emotional blocks, nor from using sexual techniques to increase your awareness, both of yourself and others.

Working with someone else in this way can double your internal awareness and help you to remove whatever blocked emotional energies either or both of you have. The focus is on how to improve your awareness of your own internal emotional energy as it relates to your inner self. Often at this point a person who has not previously been capable of intimacy finds they have been enabled to let go of doubts and fears and have learned to trust someone else. The more adept you become in dealing with your own essential energy the easier it becomes to share, interestingly enough often without the use of the physical sexual act.

In theory, moving along the path towards one's own Tao should be easy; a simple blending of two energy fields to make a larger more powerful one. In practice it can become a lot more difficult and a simple demonstration shows why. Think of these two energy fields as quite sensitive and tender. Rather like two sticky horse chestnuts, their 'hooks' (individual past experiences) can become tangled up with one another and their relationship becomes a reactive one. Literally they react to one another's difficulties and end up hurt and confused.

The able Taoist practitioner will recognize that this is simply a stage to be gone through and will face whatever demons and ghosts arise because of it. The most common manifestation of these demons is to have to deal with old family trauma and their effects. It has become the fashion in Western psychotherapy to 'forgive one's parents'. In essence, this probably means understanding the forces which have made them who they are. As such old stuff comes to the surface it is more than possible to get caught up in what a few years ago was labelled 'false memory syndrome' and to assume past injury and abuse.

The Taoist practitioner will usually recognize these feelings and emotions as they come up as illusion and will set about, using the techniques he has learned, dissolving them and letting them go. Remembering that they have inherited those forces they will set about minimizing their effect in him. In Taoist practice this is known as 'facing the internal demons' and obviously having a sensitive partner who is aware of the process can help tremendously. In meditative practice this can be a very difficult stage and Kumar Frantzis calls it 'jumping into the dragon's mouth'. Just as a child will suffer from nightmares if he has not been able to come to terms with what has happened during the day, so in meditation the fear and terror must arise in order for you to deal with it. One advantage of the meditative state is, however, that you are in a state of awareness and therefore can monitor what is going on. There is no need to allow oneself to be trapped. You can 'stop the tape' at any time and can come back to it whenever necessary. For the Westerner, creative visualization can be of great help, particularly if you choose to use the symbols and forms from Taoist legend and practice.

Returning for a moment to the Microcosmic Orbit as a very simple way of circulating the energy, as you learn more you can use this technique to cleanse and clear your mental energy as much as you do your physical. Your ultimate aim is to convert *Chi* into spirit (*shen*) so the idea is to reach the centre of your being, achieving emptiness and tranquillity. The Taoist practitioner recognizes that this is an ongoing process which can take years and is prepared to be patient with himself and others.

Because Taoist meditation is fully in accord with Nature and Nature is sometimes active and sometimes quiescent, it would be a misuse of the energy to use it purely for oneself, as a means of stress-management or simply as a form of relaxation. If the practitioner sets out with only that in mind, then he will find himself getting stuck and very frustrated. One of the most important lessons at this stage is to allow the energy to flow 'like water'; if the energy flows then so does everything else.

> Who accepts nature's flow becomes all-cherishing;
> Being all-cherishing he becomes impartial;
> Being impartial he becomes magnanimous;
> Being magnanimous he becomes natural;
> Being natural he becomes one with the Way;
> Being one with the Way he becomes immortal:
> Though his body will decay, the Way will not.
>
> The Way is limitless,

So nature is limitless,
So the world is limitless,
And so I am limitless.

Now the practitioner starts dealing with mind and thought. At this level you are moving deeper into where thoughts come from. You have dealt with the cellular level, having done your best to 'recreate' your body; now it is time to recreate your mind.

You have worked with the energy lines in your body and now it is important that you begin to work with the connections between your mind and the new body you have created. In fact this is an exercise in making everything One, it simply recognises the component parts. It is well known that the mind makes a poor servant and a bad master and the way to bring this under control is to create a discipline for yourself. This means taking responsibility for your own being, and it requires you to recognise that emotions can prevent you from becoming 'mature'.

Spending time linking the energy in the body, seeing aches and pains as emotional blockages, often means that you are able to perceive how your emotions can have you standing in your own light and causing yourself problems. An extension of this is recognizing how you deliberately pull problems inward. At this point you are not making those problems for yourself — you have just become a very fertile ground for them to happen.

Just as the world had to learn how to deal with the negative effects of the atom bomb, so the practitioner has to learn how to deal with what might be called 'the art of negative manifestation.' This then comes down to the efficient use of one's chi and energy. It is very wearing to have to keep creating blocks against what is coming towards us and indeed working in this way might be considered a form of masochism – the victim mentality. Besides which it means that you are simply transferring your instinctive defensive techniques outside the body to the *Chi* body.

It is much better to learn the process of manifestation, how things come into being and what part, if any, you need to play in that process. Learning not to be attached to results is an important pa t of the progress towards the Tao, and while some of your initial attempts at making things happen may be absolutely disastrous, as you perceive that this is not magic, but living within the Tao, the process becomes more natural and easier.

This stage is often called the psychic stage and it is vital that you do not get caught up in it and its manifestations. At this stage the art of clairvoyance occurs quite naturally, as also does the ability to know and understand where people are coming from. Getting sidetracked into this particular cul-de-sac though does not help one's own personal development or the journey towards Tao. Moving beyond this stage means that not only are you taking responsibility for your body and your emotions, but you are also verging on the art of personal alchemy called nei-dan. This is the art of personal transformation, changing the baser energies within into finer subtle power.

For the Taoist *nei-dan* is about finding the secret of life, of refining the energies to the point where everything takes on a luminous quality and becomes the energy of light. The practitioner refines his own energy, learns to channel it effectively, learns the art of *wu-wei* (not having to take action) and moves in to a place of emptiness.

> If you share this wealth, doing what you want for yourself with as many people or situations as possible, you find that you personally will do a lot better. You will create a much finer world in which to live. Finer not only for yourself but for everybody who is there with you. This becomes a pretty important issue whose implications reach far past surface meaning.

Chapter Nine

THOUGHTS AND IDEAS

Practising the exercises in this chapter will probably give you a
different concept of your own being.
The quotes that have been selected are those which hopefully
will confirm that feeling for you, give you pause for thought and
allow you to understand Tao more fully.

I have no desires
And the people find their original mind.

If a man fails to have a firm hold of virtue and has no firm faith in
the Tao, what account can be made of him if he lives? What
account can be made of him if he dies?

When a man's physical body is not straight he feels dissatisfied
and seeks to fix it. But when his mind is not straight he doesn't
feel dissatisfaction. This is called ignorance of the relative
importance of things.

Those who have abandoned their desires:
Observe your mind by introspection -
And see there is no mind.
Then observe the body,
Look at yourself from without -
And see there is no body.
Then observe others by glancing out afar -
And see there are no beings.
Once you have realised these three,
You observe emptiness!
The Taoist Experience by Liva Kohn

Only when a man of worth has himself been enlightened does he try to enlighten others. Nowadays however, one tries to enlighten others while oneself is in darkness.

The word "enlightenment" seems to be a translation of the German "Aufklaerung". I think it came into Western usage because Schopenhauer got to Buddhism before any sane person did. "Enlightenment" is not the literal translation of any classical Buddhist term. There is plenty of light imagery in Buddhism, of course, especially in Mahayana. As you know, "amitaabha" means "possessing unmeasured light". But the term usually mistranslated as "enlightenment" is "bodhi", which is better translated as "knowledge, understanding, intellect". It can also be rendered as "being awake" or "awareness". Being awake, of course, is something than can be done even in the dark, so it has nothing to do with enlightenment. So my advice is to stop using that term. It only confuses people and makes them think that Buddhism was the product of 18th century European thinking.
Richard P. Hayes

Chapter Nine

A certain Sun Xui appeared at the gate of Master Bian Quingzi to pay him a call. "When I was living in the village" he said "No-one ever said I lacked good conduct. When I faced difficulty no-one ever said I lacked courage. Yet when I worked the fields, it never seemed to be a good year for crops, and when I served the ruler, it never seemed to be a good time for advancement. So I am an outcast from the villages, an exile from the towns. What crime have I committed against Heaven? Why should I meet this fate?"

Master Bian said, "Have you never heard how the Perfect Man conducts himself? He forgets his liver and gall and thinks no more about his eyes and ears. Vague and aimless, he wanders beyond the dirt and dust; free and easy, tending to nothing is his job. This is what is called 'doing but not looking for any thanks, bringing up but not bossing.' II Now you show off your wisdom in order to astound the ignorant, work at your good conduct in order to distinguish yourself from the disreputable, going around bright and shining as though you were carrying the sun and moon in your hand! You've managed to keep your body in one piece, you have all the ordinary nine openings, you haven't been struck down midway by blindness or deafness, lameness or deformity – compared to a lot of people, you're a lucky man. How do you have any time to go around complaining against Heaven. Be on your way!. After Master Sun had left, Master Bian went back into his house, sat down for a while, and then looked up to heaven an sighed. One of his disciples asked, "Why does my teacher sigh?

Master Bian said, "Just now Sun Xiu came to see me, and described to him the virtue of the Perfect Man. I'm afraid he was very startled and may end up in a complete muddle."

"Surely not," said the disciple "Was what Master Sun said right and what my teacher said wrong) If so then wrong can certainly never make a muddle out of night Or was what Master Sun right and what my master said wrong. If so, then he must have been in a muddle when he came here, so what's the harm.?

When Confucius visited Chu, Jie Yu, the madman of Chu, wandered by his gate crying, "Phoenix, phoenix, how has virtue failed! The future you cannot wait for; the past you cannot pursue. When the world has the Way, the sage succeeds; when the world is without the Way, the sage survives. In times like the present, we do well to escape penalty. Good fortune is light as a feather, but nobody knows how to pick it up. Misfortune is heavy as the earth, but nobody knows how to stay out of its way. Leave off, leave off – this teaching men virtue! Dangerous, dangerous to mark off the ground and run! Fool, fool – don't spoil my walking! I walk a crooked way – don't step on my feet. The mountain trees do themselves harm; the grease in the torch burns itself up. The cinnamon can be eaten and so it gets cut down; the lacquer tree can be used and so it gets hacked apart. All men know the use of the useful, but nobody knows the use of the useless!"

Conclusion:

Your Tao

Those who choose to follow and study Tao literally choose a Way that enables them to explore Life in a way that suits their own personality. They can explore it in a structured or unstructured way.

In dividing the study of Tao, as so many do, into the philosophy or religion 'of Tao' we actually fall into the trap of making a duality of something which is One and One only, thus putting ourselves in an either/or situation. When we go one stage further and decide to study the religion or philosophy of Taoism we have moved considerably further away from the truth of Tao. If, however, we define philosophy as the study of motivating concepts or principles, and religion as a cause, principle or activity pursued with zeal, then it might be said that we are pursuing with zeal the motivating concept of Tao. This immediately means that we have become aware of part of the meaning of Tao and have begun to 'get hold of it'.

In many ways, the principle is an easy one to understand. Observation shows that there has to be a motivating (moving) force behind everything, which cannot be given a name because that would limit it and give it boundaries. Tao is unchanging, and pervades everything. It only moves or makes changes when absolutely necessary, and then expresses itself in numerous ways, each expression correct within itself, yet always with the potential to change.

Conclusion

This potential for change, cyclical in character, gives rise to growth and decay particularly in the natural world. (That natural world exists because of the polarity between heaven and earth, light and shade, *yin* and *yang*.) As human beings we must learn to understand that polarity and learn to handle it without interfering with it. The sage or wise man understands that he has his place within the cosmic order of things and that to become Perfect Man he must adhere to his own principles.

> He who knows the part which the Heavenly in him plays, and knows also that which the Human in him ought to play, has reached the perfection of knowledge.

It is knowing the part which the human 'ought to play' which can so often cause us problems. If we are truly in touch with Tao – the Ultimate – our conduct will be above reproach. Unfortunately, by our very nature we are not at first constantly in touch. We must learn how to retain our links and that requires that we understand the principles of self-management. This means understanding the principle of conserving ching, basic life essence, in order to give rise to *chi*, vital energy. *Chi* when used properly becomes refined into *shen* which is spirit. Moving through the realms of spirit means that you achieve Emptiness since all illusion falls away. This is *Wu* which ultimately yields to Tao, Supreme Ultimatelessness.

These are processes which need to be gone through, sometimes in sequence and sometimes together, in order to reach our full potential. This is where our own personalities must come to the fore. Our life experiences will have formed our characters and as a result there will be some behaviours which we must learn and some we must unlearn.

> If you work by the Way,
> you will be of the Way;
> If you work through its virtue
> you will be given the virtue;

Abandon either one
and both abandon you.

This means being true to ourselves and doing the best we can in the circumstances in which we find ourselves. According to the Tao this requires that you first discover if action is necessary or if non-action is more appropriate. While the ideal is non-doing, temperamentally we are not all suited to this and so we must work out how we react or respond to situations – find out what is our pattern. Once we know this, we can make the necessary adjustments, though we may not always achieve non-action. We do become aware however of how we use our energy, and what a precious commodity it is. This often has the effect of loosening old tensions , clearing pain we have held on to for some time and allowing us to drop bad habits. We begin to discover the three treasures of the Tao, wisdom, knowledge and understanding.

As the energy within us becomes freer and the blocks in our physical and emotional systems begin to dissolve or be cleared, we can begin to use the same techniques used by the ancients to have the energy made more available to us. Learning to circulate it using *Chi Gung* or meditative techniques opens the door to the realms of spirit and spiritual energy.

At this stage we do have to be a little circumspect. The realms of the spirit are seductive, and it is easy to be sidetracked into a type of fascination with the magical showier aspects of the Tao. Again, how we respond to the needs of this learning experience will depend on our character, but if we appreciate that it is all a question of balance we should not come to any harm.

Rituals, ceremonies and scriptures are a most important aspect of this stage and much can be learned by studying the rituals which have built up a great deal of power since they were first inaugurated at the beginning of Taoism. We learn that the art of transformation is to be applied on a personal level – that we are capable of transforming our cruder physical *Chi* into a more refined *Shen* or spiritual energy which then allows us to be in contact with other energies in all dimensions of a like vibration.

Conclusion

We will no doubt become aware that our requirements within the material world are changing, perhaps that we no longer crave sensation or material goods. In some ways, life becomes simpler and we feel that we are more 'in the flow'. Because of this, good things happen as if by magic and we are more able to deal with the more negative aspects of living. As we move through this stage, we may come to the realization that life and death are all one:

Holding to the Great Form
All pass away.
They pass away unharmed, resting in Great Peace.

Shen energy also means that we begin to have a wider perspective on life, that often the Taoist arts begin to have more meaning. *Feng Shui*, the art of placement, becomes more meaningful as does calligraphy and painting, not just as adornment but also as a personal expression of creativity. Dance, movement and symbolism all open up new avenues for exploration, and we may find that we are surprised at the amount of energy and power we have available to us with which to explore such things. It is as though we find ourselves on a path that many have trodden before us, with admittance to a whole new body of knowledge. We have access to the wisdom of others – including the ancestors or those who have gone before – and the power that it brings. Now we have the ability to 'go where the wind takes us' and explore the Ten Thousand expressions of Tao.

The Westerner, who has hitherto not had access to the same cultural heritage as the Chinese, may have to learn a different way of thinking, not in straight lines, nor in terms of cause and effect, but in a more circular manner, understanding the rise and fall of natural energy. As he becomes more efficient at being able to judge this, he will come to appreciate the principle of Emptiness or *wu*. Emptiness is not an easy concept to understand, and the majority of people find it difficult to practise.

As we have learned to adjust our energies and become aware of their power and fullness so we must become aware of their emptiness, not in the sense of having no power (being powerless) but more in the sense of not needing to have power. Where there is emptiness there is always room for something to happen – or not as the case may be. Also, where there is emptiness, this can be preserved in full measure; this is where meditation can come into its own. By preserving tranquillity we are able to 'do everything'.

> In studying, each day something is gained.
> In following the Tao, each day something is lost.
> Lost and again lost.
> Until there is nothing left to do.
> Not-doing, nothing is left undone

Finally, when the art of not-doing has been perfected, there is Tao. We have seen that this is indescribable and also that it is formless. Here we come up against a conundrum. If something is formless then how can we experience it; if something is indescribable then how can we describe it? The answer is we don't.

Knowing that it is there, knowing that we do not grasp it or need to grasp it means that we are actually 'in it'. All we need to do to remain in it – at least while we are within the physical realm – is to become the sage, or the Wise Person. This means acting appropriately under all circumstances, helping others when necessary and simply 'being'. It is at this stage that we have the ability to apply some of the alchemical practices that were considered to be so important in ancient times.

Now, however, we apply them as internal alchemy, refining and refining our energy to the point where we can become 'immortal'. This does *not* mean living forever, but does mean recognizing our ability to exist forever in a non-corporeal sense. Our energy eventually will no longer need the outer covering of the physical body but simply becomes itself and can 'be'. This does not presuppose a life after death, simply that we are in the Tao and are not separate from it. We are both part of the Way and the Way itself.

Conclusion

The Personal Path

There is no beginning to the study of Tao and equally no end. There is, however, a point of entry, and there are as many points of entry as there are people. You do not have to be religious, nor do you have to study philosophy; above anything else you do have to be curious. For most people the best point of entry is the scripture known as the *Tao Te Ching*.

One way of initially approaching the whole subject is to read the scriptures almost as poetry, and simply appreciate them in that way. Most often this will spark off various thoughts, ideas or concepts which you will wish to follow up. Here you can be truly like the butterfly in Chuang Tse's dream (or for that matter the sages of old) and go Wandering About until you have found an aspect to absorb you. Now you can spend as much time as you like on each aspect and will often find that your interest has led you into other areas. You might find that you want to study other ancient scriptures, Eastern religions, Western Philosophy, martial arts: the list is endless. Let your intuition be your guide, but always be prepared to remain open and open-minded. Recognize too that learning does not only come from books, but comes from living and experiencing, so each occurrence is an opportunity to live fully within the scheme of things, to be present in the moment. Here you might also ask the questions:

What does this mean to me?
What does this mean to others?
What does this mean to the visible world?

You are literally now on the Way. It has been suggested that this Tao is like a path – there are no turn-offs, only lay-bys. Each of those lay-bys is complete within itself, so if you find yourself following a course of action without quite understanding what is going on, stop and listen to yourself. Listen to your body, listen to your emotions and listen to your spirit – your inner self. Ask yourself what they are telling you, what they need.

Often you will find that you need to adopt some form of bodily or mental discipline, and at this point it is worthwhile at least exploring the exercise systems that the ancients discovered worked for them. The mind-set for this type of workout is different to the activity-based Western approach. *Tai Chi Chuan*, as we have seen, mimics the natural world and *Chi Gung* allows us to monitor and channel our natural energy. Whether you work with the more Fire-based martial arts or the more flowing Water-based forms is a matter of personal choice and temperament.

You may well become disillusioned by some of the external manifestations of Tao as you embark on your journey, but be wise enough to let this disillusionment go, for what others make of their portion of life is not your concern, except perhaps where you are able to be of assistance. Again this does not suggest being indifferent, it is simply accepting things as they are. We are all individuals and will find our own Way. As you release your blocks to progress you will no doubt find yourself becoming more tolerant of your own and others' idiosyncrasies and belief systems.

All belief systems have developed their own rituals and ceremonies and none is richer than the Taoist religion. The four animals, Dragon, Phoenix, Tortoise and Tiger all have symbolism and meaning for the Chinese mind, being guardians of the four directions. Once that symbolism is understood, you may wish to incorporate them into your own rituals and prayers.

An interesting exercise is to discover which of the four you relate most strongly to and to work for a time with the power of that animal in your everyday life. The most obvious application is in *Feng Shui* and in the correct placement of these animals, but you might like to extend your knowledge by using them as helpers or meditative aids. You might use the tortoise as a symbol of stability when tackling a difficult task, for instance, or the power of the dragon when needing an extra boost of energy.

Morning and evening rites, if you choose to adopt them, will give you fixed points throughout the day to enable you to reconfirm your dedication to the path you have chosen. There are many Internet sites now which have versions of suitable scriptures for your contemplation and some which give you the correct pronunciation of the prayers. There are also sites that have suitable musical accompaniments for your meditations. Other festivals which are important to the Taoist can also be explored in this way.

It is at this point in your journey that you may come up against something of an oddity. By and large, people tend to classify themselves as a way of confirming their own identity. Thus you might say 'I am Taoist', ' I study Tao', 'I follow the Tao' among other things. In fact, you probably will come to the conclusion that you can claim none of these things, nor is there any need to do so. If you have made a commitment to living life in the most effective way possible without 'doing' you have probably become (or are doing) all of the above, but have no need to put a label on them or classify them. This is the beginning of *Wu* (Emptiness) you are 'in the Tao' and everything is as it should be.

Now is the point at which you recognize that the rest of your existence is going to be about transformation – personal transformation initially, but then transformation in the truest sense of the word: 'changing the nature, state or condition of your being' as appropriate. At the same time will you accept the unchanging nature of Being and have truly found your personal path within Tao. We leave you as we began with the words of Lao Tse:

> *Stand before it and there is no beginning.*
> *Follow it and there is no end.*
> *Stay with the ancient Tao,*
> *Move with the present.*

Bibliography

Chronicles of Tao, the secret life of a Taoist master Deng, Ming-Dao, Harper San Francisco, 1993 ISBN 0062502190

Chuang Tzu, The Inner Chapters A.C. Graham et al, Unwin, 1986 ISBN 0042990130

Complete Illustrated Guide to Chinese Medicine Tom Williams Ph.D., Element Books, 1996 ISBN 1-85230-881-8

Dictionary of Asian Philosophies St Elmo Nauman Jr., Routledge & Kegan Paul, London, 1979 ISBN 0 415 03971 1

Facets of Taoism, Essays in Chinese religion Holmes Welch (ed.), Yale University Press, 1979 ISBN 0 300026730

Psychedelic Prayers after the Tao te ching Timothy Leary, Poets Press, 1966 ISBN W000024865

The Encyclopaedia of Religion (Volume 14) Mircea Eliade (Editor in Chief), Macmillan, New York, 1987 ISBN 0 002 909850 5

Bibliography

Tao te Ching, the book of meaning and life Translation and commentary by Richard Wilhelm, Arkana, 1985 ISBN 1850630119

Tao – the Watercourse Way Alan Watts, Penguin Books, 1979 ISBN 0140221549

Taoism, the way of the Mystic Cooper, J. C., Crucible, 1990 ISBN 185274071X

The eight immortals of Taoism Eds. Kwok Man Ho and Joanne O'Brien, Rider Books, 1990 ISBN 0712636455

The Elements of Taoism Martin Palmer, Element Books, 1991 ISBN 1852302313

The essential Tao, An initiation into the heart of Taoism through the authentic Tao Te Ching and the inner teachings of Chuang-tzu Thomas Cleary, Harper Collins, 1992 ISBN 0062501623

The Feng Shui Handbook Derek Waters, Thorsons, 1995 ISBN 0 85030 959 X

The Religion of China, Confucianism & Taoism Max Weber The Free Press, 1968 ISBN 0029344506

The Rider Encyclopaedia of Eastern Philosophy and Religion Edited by Stephan Schumacher and Gert Woerner, Rider Books, 1989 ISBN 0 7126 7097 1

The Spiritual teachings of the Tao Mark Forstater, Hodder & Stoughton, 2001, ISBN 0340733209

The Tao of Management Bob Messing, Wildwood House, 1989 ISBN 0 7045 0631 9

The Tao of Physics Fritjof Capra, Wildwood House, 1975 ISBN 0704501422

Bibliography

The Tao of Pooh and the Teh of Piglet Benjamin Hoff. Methuen, 1994 ISBN 0 413 69160 8

The tao teh ching, translated by James Legge, Grange, c2001 ISBN 1840134739

The Wisdom of China Lin Yutang (ed.), Michael Joseph, 1944

The Worlds Religions: A Completely Revised and Updated Edition of The Religions of Man Smith, Houston, HarperCollins, 1991

Understanding Taoism Origins, beliefs, practices, holy texts, sacred places, Jennifer Oldstone-Moore, Duncan Baird, 2003 ISBN 1904292577

Understanding world religions, Hinduism, Buddhism, Taoism, Confucianism, Judaism, Islam George W Braswell, Broadman & Holman, 1994 ISBN 0 805 41068 6

Zhuangzui Basic Writings translated by Burton Watson, Columbia University Press, 2003 ISBN 0 231 12959 9

Web Sites

Should I have inadvertently omitted to include any website I have used I unreservedly apologise and acknowledge my indebtedness to them

http://www.chinatown-online.co.uk/pages/culture/beliefs.html

http://www.alchemywebsite.com/chinese.html

http://www.taoistarts.net/

http://www.truetao.org/enter.htm

Bibliography

http://www.chikungwebsite.fsnet.co.uk/history.htm

http://venus.unive.it/dsao/pregadio/index.html

http://ricci.rt.usfca.edu/about.html

http://www.venus.co.uk/weed/laotzu/welcome.html

http://www.eng.taoism.org.hk/glossary/eng-chi/

http://www.daozang.com/chuangtzu.html

http://www.chisuk.org.uk/bodymind/whatis/qigong.htm

http://www.cathoderaymission.freeserve.co.uk/tao/

http://helios.unive.it/~dsao/pregadio/articles/intro/intro_2.html

http://www.olsommer.com/tsoh/textonly/taoconclusion-t.html

http://www.geocities.com/Athens/Acropolis/l

http://myfengshui.geomancy.net

http://1stholistic.com/Meditation/hol_meditation_taoist_meditation.htm

http://www.coldbacon.com/chuang/chuang.html

http://www.ichingresources.co.uk/

http://www.the-tao.com/taoatlantic/meditation.html

http://www.apocryphile.net/tao/

http://www.edepot.com/taoism.shtml

http://www.clas.ufl.edu/users/gthursby/taoism

Index

Index

Index

Index